Education
for the Nation

EDUCATION
FOR THE NATION

Richard Aldrich

CASSELL

Cassell
Wellington House, 125 Strand, London WC2R 0BB
127 West 24th Street, New York, NY 10011

First published 1996

British Library Cataloguing-in-Publication Data
A catalogue record for this book is available from the British Library.

ISBN 0-304-33934-2 (hardback)
0-304-33935-0 (paperback)

Designed and typeset by Kenneth Burnley at Irby, Wirral, Cheshire.
Printed and bound in Great Britain by Redwood Books, Trowbridge, Wiltshire.

Contents

Acknowledgements

This book is the major outcome of a research project entitled 'Historical Perspectives Upon Current Educational Issues in England', funded by the Leverhulme Trust. I am most grateful to the Trust for their financial support, and to David Ingram and David Crook who not only undertook most of the contemporary and historical research but also commented upon the several drafts. My thanks are also due to Dennis Dean, Andy Green and Ronald Barnett for their most constructive criticisms, to members of MA seminar groups in History of Education at the Institute of Education, University of London and to other audiences and seminar groups at conferences and universities in Australia, Finland, the Netherlands, the United Kingdom, and the USA. Finally, I should like to express my warmest appreciation to Averil Aldrich, to Naomi Roth and her colleagues at Cassell, and to Deborah Spring, Publications Officer at the Institute, for their work in seeing the book into print.

Introduction

Education is the most important shared experience in our lives. It is so important and so all-pervasive that it is almost impossible to define. It takes place everywhere – in the family and workplace, on the bus and train, in the cinema and in front of the television set. But not all the influences which affect human beings may be called education.

Education has two key properties. The first is that it is concerned with the development of knowledge, skills and values which are generally considered to be worthwhile, or at the very least not harmful to others. For example, to teach someone to be a liar and a thief would be mis-education rather than education. The second is that education allows for participation by the person being educated, both in the process and in the outcomes. This is what distinguishes it from training (as generally conceived) and indoctrination. It is for this reason that we may speak of a person being self-educated, but not self-trained or self-indoctrinated.

The most immediately visible expression of contemporary commitment to education in this country is to be found in the formal school system. Since 1972 every child in England has received at least eleven years of compulsory schooling, and today some one-third of young people pursue full-time education beyond the age of 18. Clearly such an important feature of individual and national life should be approached in an informed, constructive and generous spirit. Education will not supply all the answers to the problems that beset us, either as individuals or as a nation, but it is the best single means of promoting intellectual, moral, physical and economic well-being. Unfortunately, in England today, education, in common with many other aspects of our lives, has become a victim of that confrontational culture which has penetrated so deeply into many facets of private and public life, including politics and the media. A classic example of such culture is to be found in the confrontational politics of Prime Minister's Question Time in the House of Commons, now relayed on television throughout the nation. While a confrontational culture may be defended as a means of guaranteeing democracy and of preserving debate and free speech, the quality of that democracy is seriously diminished if debate is characterized by assertion and counter-assertion, rather than by informed interpretation based upon evidence. The quality of democracy is also diminished if there are no agreed principles and values upon which private and public lives may be based. This is particularly true in a country such as the United Kingdom which has no written constitution and no fundamental bill of rights.

This book has a substantial purpose – to provide a basis for the restoration of informed discussion and decision-making in education. Provision of such a basis is certainly the most urgent educational task of our day. Individual attempts to improve classroom or school effectiveness will have limited success if the framework and ethos of education are flawed and subject to repeated and incoherent changes. Since 1979, and particularly since 1988, educational changes have been made as part of a wider programme to change the nature of British society. They have been driven, understandably, by the essential values of a radical revolution from the Right. The former ideal of partnership in education has been replaced by one of confrontation. Professionals have been redesignated as producers, and parents and pupils as consumers. But whilst the new competitive ethos in British life that has been generated since 1979, when Margaret Thatcher first became Prime Minister, has brought many benefits, the time is now ripe to assess, in as objective a way as possible, its gains and losses with respect to education.

This is not simply an academic exercise: it has a high purpose – to increase the understanding of education in this country. If it is successful it could be a powerful agent for good. Accordingly this book is aimed at a wide readership. Though it draws upon sound scholarship and the findings of a research project funded by the Leverhulme Trust, it is a work of popular intent. True democracy depends upon popular awareness and participation. Although it may not always be true that people get the politicians and political systems (or even the educationists and educational systems) they deserve, there is a real sense in which, in British society today, as in all democracies, ignorance is a crime.

This book originates from a query in 1993 of the then Secretary of State for Education, John Patten, who was reported as asking 'Why don't people in this country feel they own state education?' That question and many of the other key questions in respect of understanding education in England today can best be answered by historical analysis. History is the study of human events with particular reference to the dimension of time – past, present and future; it is especially concerned with change and continuity. But though the methodology of this work is historical, its nature and purposes are educational. It provides evidence and analysis about education, but it does so for the purpose of inviting the participation of the reader. There is no intention in the following pages to indoctrinate; indeed this study starts from the clear historical premise that different individuals and different societies have had, and will continue to have, different views about education. Those differences depend considerably upon cultural and economic differences: they also depend substantially upon ideological differences about what is most worthwhile in life. For example, for some it will be wealth and power; for others good works in this world and a place in a hereafter. For some the main purpose of education is to conserve; for others it is to change. Awareness of such differences naturally requires an acknowledgement that this book itself is not, and cannot be, totally objective and impartial. The writing of the history of education involves making choices and judgements which cannot be entirely value-free. But throughout the processes of research and writing great emphasis has been placed upon objective procedures, and upon giving full weight to conflicting interpretations.

Times change. At the beginning of the twentieth century British dominion extended over a quarter of the globe. One hundred years later the Empire has gone and Britain accounts for a mere one per cent of the world's population. In 1991 the country which pioneered the first industrial revolution of modern times and whose people, even in 1950, were amongst the wealthiest in the world, stood eighth in terms of standards of living among the twelve countries of the European Community, and eighteenth of the twenty-four members of the OECD. Such change has naturally been accompanied by uncertainties and generational gaps. This is reflected in many ways, for example in the confrontational culture referred to above, and in that institutions which formerly commanded widespread respect and support – monarchy, church, law, marriage – are now seen by some as partial and irrelevant.

In 1900 the educational system of England reflected its imperial role. In boys' public schools an elite band of young men were prepared to serve in the several institutions of the largest Empire the world had ever seen, and to assume the proud bearing of those whom God and good fortune had called to be masters in their own homes, in their own country, and in the world at large. The great majority of children, however, both boys and girls, attended elementary schools, where they were taught the basics of reading, writing and arithmetic, to abhor most things foreign (especially revolutions) and to be thankful that they lived in such a powerful Christian country, an island fortress indeed, guarded by an incomparable navy and ruled over by an apparently immortal queen.

Though times change, not everything changes at the same time, nor at the same speed. To situate ourselves, whether as individuals or as a nation, accurately in time is as difficult as it is potentially rewarding. Nevertheless it is a task worth undertaking. Our lives are governed as much by what happened in the past as what will happen in the future. Our journeys in the present and future will be infinitely more successful if we have as accurate as possible a map of the past. Though each human situation is unique, the record of human experience, usually referred to as history, is a rich treasure house that we neglect at our peril. Whilst a knowledge of history cannot enable us to predict the future with certainty, it provides invaluable data for choosing between different courses of action. Historical study provides an interaction with a much wider range of human experience than is possible simply by reference to the contemporary world. Those who deliberately ignore the mistakes of the past are most likely to repeat them.

The basic method employed in this book is to distinguish what is important and long lasting from that which is unimportant and transitory, to identify and explain continuities and changes, and to make judgements as to worth. This is an exercise in which we all engage in respect of our individual lives. For example, even in an age which prizes the instant and ephemeral, individuals still seek to discover those things which are of enduring importance, for example, in such areas as personal relationships and employment.

The term (and idea) of education, as used in these pages, while focusing upon formal education, also includes all those forces and agencies that are consciously employed to promote human development in respect of worthwhile activities. Similarly, evidence and analysis are drawn from a variety of human experiences. Though, as a general principle, it might be stated that evidence from nineteenth- and twentieth-century English history might be most appropriate to discussions of contemporary educational issues, on occasion contrast is as meaningful as comparison. There are many lessons to be learned from the worlds we have lost, not least about the increasing alienation of human beings from the values and rhythms associated with their natural environment.

Seven topics have been selected for investigation: access to education, curriculum, standards and assessment, teaching quality, the control of education, education and economic performance, and consumers of education. Each is examined in a separate chapter. Topics were chosen after a substantial consultation process, which included canvassing educational professionals and educational organizations, and surveying newspapers, educational journals and books. Criteria for selection included both the prominence of a particular issue in contemporary educational debate, and the extent to which such an issue has a history – that is to say a significant place in human experience that encompasses past, present and future. The order of the chapters has been arranged to follow a natural progression and to form a coherent whole. How do people get to formal education? What do they find there in terms of curriculum, standards and teaching? Who controls education and what is the relationship between education and the economy? Who are the real consumers of education and what conclusions should they draw, overall, about contemporary English education when viewed through the historical perspective? The order of treatment within a chapter is, first, to identify the dimensions of the current educational issue; second, to examine earlier manifestations of that issue; and third, to provide a framework of analysis and interpretation that covers past, present and future. Such thematic treatment means that each of the seven central chapters stands separately and is self-sufficient. The concluding chapter provides a series of overviews, and then focuses upon the issue of ownership.

Contemporary educational issues are located within an English context. The several parts of the United Kingdom – England, Scotland, Wales and Northern Ireland – have different perceptions of educational issues, and differences between their educational systems, partly as a result of their different histories. Nevertheless, all of the issues and analyses apply to some extent more broadly, both within the United Kingdom and without. Similarly there is no absolute dividing line between what is contemporary and what is historical. The Education Act of 1944, for so long heralded as the basis of the modern English educational system, no longer stands as the dividing line between past and present. More recent turning points might be James Callaghan's Ruskin College speech of 1976 which called for greater attention to be paid to financial stringency, basic skills and consumer rights; the advent to power of the first Government of Margaret Thatcher in 1979, or the Education Reform Act of 1988. More recent still was *Learning to Succeed*, the report of the Hamlyn funded National Commission on Education, published in 1993. That document represented a significant attempt to move education from a confrontational to an informed culture. This book may be regarded as a further step along that road.

ONE

Access

CURRENT ISSUES

Access may be defined as the freedom to participate in an activity, in this case education. There are many factors which determine access to education, and two broad categories may be identified.

The first is the nature and extent of educational provision available in a particular place at a particular time. Such educational provision may include both schools and other formal institutions, and other agencies like churches, clubs, libraries and sports facilities. The second category comprises such factors as wealth, social class, sex, age, race, physical and mental ability, factors which may influence an individual's ability to participate in education.

There is considerable evidence that access to, and participation in, formal education has changed markedly in recent years.

At the time of writing much political attention is being paid to increasing the supply of nursery education. All children are currently required to attend primary schools from the age of 5, and the 11-plus examination which provided the mechanism whereby children were allotted to grammar schools, secondary moderns, and a few technical or bilateral schools has been abolished in all but a few areas. More than 90 per cent of pupils aged 11 to 16 now attend secondary schools described as comprehensive. The term comprehensive, however, tends to mask a number of continuing inequalities and widely differing access opportunities. Many more pupils also stay on past the compulsory school-leaving age. In 1979 the majority of pupils left school at 16 and sought employment. By 1994 over 70 per cent of 16-year-olds continued in full-time education. Many children with special educational needs, moreover, are now integrated into mainstream schooling.

Access to independent secondary schools has been widened by the assisted places scheme. Some 80 per cent of the more than 30,000 pupils whose private school fees are publicly subsidized under the scheme come from the less wealthy groups in society – social groups C, D and E.[1]

Recent statistics of examination successes indicate that girls perform better than boys. In 1993, for example, 43 per cent of girls achieved five or more passes in GCSE at grades A to C, compared with only 34 per cent of boys; in 1994 the respective figures were 46 and 37 per cent.[2] These figures, however, have yet to be reflected in access to higher education. In 1984, 42 per cent, and in 1994 47 per cent of higher education students were female.[3]

Access to higher education has dramatically increased. Universities have proliferated with the redesignation of former polytechnics and colleges. In 1960 there were twenty-four universities; in 1994 eighty-nine. The period 1979–94 saw a doubling of student numbers, so that from that latter date some 30 per cent of the population might expect to enter higher education. In 1994 females made up nearly half of the student population and mature students one-third. In spite of such increases in numbers, however, the majority of students were still recruited from social classes A and B, which account for only one-quarter of the population. In 1992 some 67 per cent of students in the old universities, and 55 per cent in the former polytechnics came from these social groups.[4] Nevertheless, it would appear that the percentage of students recruited from social groups C, D and E is gradually increasing. Such increase has resulted in part from the provision of 'access courses' and 'return to learn' schemes offered by community and further education colleges and adult education centres. Some colleges at the older universities of Oxford and Cambridge have promoted positive discrimination in favour of pupils from inner-city state schools. The pioneering Open University continues to flourish, and flexible and distance learning approaches reinforce the belief that education is for life and not to be restricted by age, location or circumstance.

Another significant factor in respect of access is that the percentages of children from ethnic minority communities who continue into post-compulsory, full-time education, and of students from these communities who obtain degrees or other higher education qualifications, now exceed the national average.

Table 1.1: Percentages of 16- to 19-year-olds in full-time education, 1982 and 1988–90, by ethnic origin, Great Britain[5]

Ethnic group	1982		1988–90	
	men	women	men	women
White	25	24	36	38
Afro-Caribbean	26	37	39	48
South Asian	58	51	60	53

On the other hand, whilst greater provision of formal educational institutions has produced greater access overall, and seen advances amongst previously disadvantaged or underachieving groups, concerns about access remain.

Only a small minority of children attend independent schools under the assisted places scheme, yet the much greater resources of such schools, helped by tax concessions and manifested in smaller class sizes, indicate the extent to which the ability to purchase an 'independent' education still confers considerable advantages.

In January 1994 the overall pupil–teacher ratio in maintained schools was 18.1:1; in independent schools 10.3:1. Pupils in independent schools, therefore, are likely to have more chance of personal access to a teacher than those in maintained schools. Even those parents who are not able or willing to purchase an independent education for their children may still buy a house in the catchment area of a successful state school. The syndrome of neighbourhood schools is now as prevalent in England as it has long been in the United States, and estate agents regularly advertise a property as being within the catchment area of a particular secondary comprehensive or grammar school.

In spite of the undoubted development of the theory and practice of 'diversity and choice' in education since 1979, for many parents and children there is little real choice in terms of schools to attend. The Office for Standards in Education (OFSTED) and the National Commission on Education whose report, *Learning to Succeed*, was published in 1993, have both drawn attention to the particular difficulties faced by schools situated in areas where poverty is rife and unemployment high, where leisure facilities are few and criminal activities flourish. Low expectations, sometimes combined with poor teaching, further reduce the self-esteem and ambitions of pupils, and restrict their achievements.[6] It has been argued that rather than providing a few escape routes for a small minority of pupils, and rescue squads for a handful of establishments whose standards are quite unacceptable, the urgent problems faced by many inner-city (and other) schools can only be solved by treating such schools as the 'educational equivalent of enterprise zones'.[7]

Substantial problems still remain about many of the figures of improved access. Although post-16 participation rates have dramatically improved, three serious questions may be asked about this phenomenon. The first is to what extent this is a product of government policy, especially the introduction of the GCSE, or rather the effect of juvenile unemployment and the decline of apprenticeship. The second is whether there is an appropriate curriculum or range of qualifications for those who stay on at school post-16 and who are not attracted to the GCE 'A'-level and higher education route. The third is that by some international standards participation rates post-16 are still lamentably low. In 1991 the percentage of 16–19-year-olds in full-time education and training in Britain was 56, compared to 88 in Germany and France, and 94 in Japan.[8] As to access to higher education, a report from the Council for Industry and Higher Education showed that in 1991 three high-quality GCE 'A'-level passes, the traditional 'passport' to higher education, remained out of the reach of more than 90 per cent of pupils in secondary comprehensive schools.

Problems also appear to exist in respect of the competitive ethos which underlies recent government approaches to education. There is no evidence that countries with the highest educational standards encourage market competition within their school systems, and competition of necessity produces winners and losers. In the industrial and commercial marketplace unsuccessful companies go to the wall and their employees lose their jobs, and the same market forces apply in respect of independent schools. Whether such forces can, or should, be extended to all maintained schools remains highly problematic. One difficulty is that the dice are so heavily loaded in favour of certain educational institutions that greater differentiation may emerge, differentiation based upon socio-economic power. To those who have, more may be given. Maintained schools in wealthier areas have more access to supplementary funding from parents, and such funds may be used not only to purchase extra equipment and facilities, but also to employ extra teachers. In the sphere of higher education the universities and colleges of Oxford and Cambridge, with their historic prestige and inherited wealth, have much greater access to private financial sources than the newer universities; for example, Oxford University raised £328 million in six years. As with institutions, so with students. The recent shift from mandatory grants towards loans has been most damaging to students from less wealthy homes. In 1994 the average student could expect to be some £2,000 in debt at the end of a first-degree course, a figure that will undoubtedly increase as loans acquire an even greater prominence.[9] Of course it can be argued that higher education is an investment, and that many people take out loans to buy goods which may be regarded as luxuries rather than necessities. Nevertheless, those universities which traditionally recruit a high proportion of students from independent schools, and whose parents are accustomed to paying for the education of their offspring – Oxford, Cambridge, Bristol, Durham, Exeter – are less likely to experience problems from students whose capacity for work is diminished by financial pressures.

Another access problem that arises from the application of market principles to schools concerns the position of children with behavioural, emotional, physical or learning difficulties. In the 1980s there was a policy of placing such children in mainstream, rather than in special schools, and thus improving their access. The ethos of the marketplace, however, has caused both schools and local education authorities to reconsider policies of integration. Not only may 'statemented' children incur higher costs than other children, they are also less likely to perform as well in the Standard Assessment Tasks and external examinations upon which schools are being judged. Recent evidence that more than 12 per cent of children excluded from schools have special needs has raised the fear that schools 'are unable or unwilling to keep them'.[10]

Two final comments may be made in respect of gender and race. While it may be true that female pupils and students are now enjoying considerably improved access to examination successes, their limited participation and achievement in such areas as science, technology and computer studies still gives rise for concern. Nor have they, as yet, made significant inroads into many areas of employment, including the senior common rooms of Oxford and Cambridge. At Cambridge only a quarter of the tutors and 5 per cent of the professors are women. The corresponding figures for Oxford are fourteen and 3 per cent.[11] Women represent only 2 per cent of members of large company boards, 3 per cent of surgeons, 8 per cent of architects and 9 per cent of MPs.[12] Similarly, in spite of the achievements of some children and students from ethnic minority communities, there is continuing evidence of problems of access for others. The failure of the government to extend funding to Moslem schools on the same terms as Christian ones may be taken as one example. A second concerns the National Curriculum. It has been argued that the Education Reform Act of 1988 has 'actively erected boundaries around a white, Christian, Eurocentric curriculum that is geared towards underpinning British culture and preventing it from being "swamped".'[13]

In conclusion, therefore, there are two clear positions in respect of access to education. The one points to figures of improved participation overall, and amongst females and those from ethnic minorities. The other questions both the nature and extent of such changes, and argues that in the long run the application to education of the principles of market forces and choice and diversity will decrease, rather than increase, equality of access.

HISTORICAL PERSPECTIVES

Access to education is a most complex issue, and there have been significant changes in emphasis over time. For example, for more than three hundred years following the Protestant Reformation of the sixteenth century, adherence to a particular form of Christianity was a prerequisite for access to many educational institutions. In 1996 the emphasis is rather upon equality of access for adherents of faiths other than Christianity. Lack of space precludes a detailed examination of all the issues, but two which have been of central importance over many years are examined here: social class and gender.

Social class

For centuries children and young people have been educated principally in accordance with their positions in society. For example, in the medieval period the education of the knight and landowner would have been very different from that of the cleric or peasant. Some parts of that education would have been received in a family, others in an occupational setting. In some instances, for example those of a medieval guild master or an eighteenth-century handloom weaver, there might have been little, if any, difference between the two contexts. Schools and colleges were a means of preparation for clerical occupations. For example in the 1380s William of Wykeham, Bishop of Winchester, founded both Winchester College and New College, Oxford. The first was intended for 'seventy poor and needy scholars'; the second for 'seventy poor scholars, clerks, to study theology, canon and civil law and arts'. Nevertheless both at Winchester and at Eton (founded in 1440 by Henry VI for twenty-five poor and needy scholars) such pupils were soon joined by fee-paying sons of the gentry and nobility. A similar development occurred at the colleges of Oxford and Cambridge. While the clerical connections of the two English universities continued into the twentieth century, for centuries they also served as finishing schools for the sons of the wealthy and influential.

During the nineteenth century access to education, and more specifically to schooling, continued to be determined by social class. Indeed the connections between types of schools and social class increased, as local customs gave way to national arrangements. Three royal commissions, Newcastle, 1861, Clarendon, 1864 and Taunton, 1868, reported on schools for the poor, wealthy and middling classes and, in so doing, confirmed the social distinctions between them. At a time when schooling was neither compulsory nor free, the Newcastle report acknowledged that elementary schooling for the poor – religion, reading, writing and arithmetic – would be an end in itself. The Revd James Fraser reported to the Newcastle Commissioners that:

> Even if it were possible, I doubt whether it would be desirable, with a view to the real interests of the peasant boy, to keep him at school till he was 14 or 15 years of age. But it is not possible. We must make up our minds to see the last of him, as far as day school is concerned, at 10 or 11. We must frame our system of education upon this hypothesis; and I venture to maintain that it is quite possible to teach a child soundly and thoroughly, in a way that he shall not forget it, all that is necessary for him to possess in the shape of intellectual attainments, by the time he is 10 years old.[14]

Children of the poor had always worked from an early age, although in rural communities such work might have been more seasonal in nature than it would be in the urban areas and industrialized society of nineteenth-century England. Children, like their parents, understood the need for them to contribute to the family wage as soon as was possible. Improved access to elementary schooling came with the provision of schools under the Elementary Education Act of 1870. Under the terms of this Act school boards were established in areas where school provision was insufficient in terms of quantity or quality. This exercise in 'filling up the gaps' was so successful that compulsory school attendance to the age of 10 was introduced in 1880, to be raised to 11 in 1893 and 12 in 1899. In 1895 only 14 per cent of children in elementary schools were aged 12 or over, and this figure included a significant number of reluctant attenders who had been unable to reach the educational standard necessary to secure their release. In 1891 elementary schooling was made free. The school-leaving age was raised to 14 in 1918, 15 in 1947 and 16 in 1972.

While most commentators would see compulsory schooling and the raising of the school-leaving age as laudable developments, it should be noted that the concept of access includes a dimension of freedom in participation. Although, theoretically, children might be educated in ways other than in elementary schools, in practical terms the ministrations of school boards, attendance committees and attendance officers meant that access to other forms of education was substantially diminished, if not completely denied. State direction of elementary education, both at central and local levels, was undertaken by members of the middling and upper classes. In consequence the curricula and ethos of elementary schools reflected the aims and ambitions of such classes for the children who attended these schools, rather than those of the children themselves or their parents. They were, indeed, primary instruments of social control. An alternative, and more popular means of education was thereby eliminated. For example, the report of the Newcastle Commission showed that more than half a million children of working-class parents attended private schools. The decline and demise of the private working-class school during the second half of the nineteenth century has been little known and less lamented. Nevertheless, in the context of access to education these schools represented an important alternative to the education provided under the auspices of Church and state. Although the majority of private schools were probably inferior in terms of qualified teachers, premises and equipment to those supported by religious societies or school boards, they did provide a form of education responsive to the rhythms and needs of working-class life.

Although elementary schooling was in practice and intent an education in itself, rather than preparatory to further schooling, it did furnish one, albeit limited, means of modest social advancement. This was the pupil teacher system, established in 1846 by the Committee of Council, whereby some pupils could undertake a five-year apprenticeship, teaching in the school and receiving further tuition from the master or mistress at the end of the day. Some pupil teachers proceeded directly into teaching, others to training college, others again to occupations other than teaching.

Whereas the Newcastle Commission had investigated the education of more than two million children, in 1864 the Clarendon Commission reported on a mere nine schools: Eton, Winchester, Charterhouse, Harrow, Rugby, Westminster and Shrewsbury, together with the two day schools of Merchant Taylors' and St Paul's. These were the 'great schools', historic institutions with national reputations. They were soon to be emulated, if not surpassed, by a crop of new foundations, many with specific professional connotations: Epsom for the sons of doctors; Marlborough for the sons of clergy; Wellington for the sons of army officers. By the end of the nineteenth century the term 'public school' was being applied to more than a hundred institutions. In terms of numbers, therefore, access to public schools greatly increased, particularly as these schools restricted themselves to older pupils, younger boys being catered for in the new preparatory schools. But such access was restricted to the sons of the professional, middle and upper classes. Indeed schools became more socially exclusive than before. During the nineteenth century founders' requirements in respect of the free admission of local poor boys were frequently set aside, once more supposedly in the 'real interests' of the poor themselves.

Though the Clarendon Commissioners called attention to several faults, their confidence in these nine establishments and in their products was expressed in glowing terms:

> It is not easy to estimate the degree in which the English people are indebted to these schools for the qualities on which they pique themselves the most – for their capacity to govern others and control themselves, their aptitude for combining freedom with order, their public spirit, their vigour and manliness of character, their strong but not slavish respect for public opinion, their love of healthy sports and exercise. These schools have been the chief nurseries of our statesmen . . . and they have had perhaps the largest share in moulding the character of an English gentleman.[15]

That perception has continued until today. In England, boys' public schools are still the chief nurseries of statesmen and of others in power, whether in government, commerce and industry, or the professions. Access to them, apart from a relatively small number of assisted places, is still restricted to the sons (and some of the daughters) of the wealthy.

The Taunton Commission, which had the unenviable task of reporting on all the schools not covered by Newcastle and Clarendon, identified three grades of boys' school. The first included those, like Uppingham, that were already developing into public schools. Other characteristics of first-grade schools were that their pupils would be substantially drawn from the upper middle and professional classes. Many would stay at school until the age of 18, and some would proceed to the universities. Second-grade schools would cater for pupils to 16 years of age, and provide a modified classical education for those intending to enter business and commerce, or a variety of professional occupations. Third-grade schools were intended for the sons of lesser farmers, tradespeople and others who would not wish their sons to mix with children of ordinary folk in the elementary school.

Of course schools did not, and would not, fit neatly into such categories, and although in some senses the Taunton Report confirmed the relationship between social class and schooling, it also recommended some reorganization of school endowments with a view to widening access by the provision of some free and assisted places.

Elementary schooling for all was achieved by the end of the nineteenth century, to be followed by secondary schooling for all in the twentieth. By the end of the last century there were 'upthrusts' from the elementary school system in the shape of higher grade and higher elementary schools, many of which taught science for the purpose of obtaining grants from the Science and Art Department. But the Education Act of 1902 established maintained grammar schools on a traditional pattern. Although at first the majority of pupils in these schools were fee paying, free places or scholarships were provided for bright children from elementary schools. By 1907 more than half the pupils in grant-aided secondary schools had previously attended elementary schools, and a quarter paid no fees. By 1937 three-quarters of pupils in aided and maintained secondary schools were former elementary school pupils. A ladder of educational opportunity had been provided which allowed the children of working-class parents access to an academic secondary schooling and even to university.

Two influential voices of the 1920s were those of R. H. Tawney and Kenneth Lindsay. In 1922 in *Secondary Education for All*, Tawney argued that:

> What we require is to recognize boldly that nothing less than general secondary education will either stand the criticism of the educationalists, or satisfy the demands of a working class that has tasted the tree of knowledge and does not intend that its children should be fobbed off with educational shoddy which was foisted upon itself. In place, in short, of 'elementary' education for nine-tenths of the children and 'secondary' education for the exceptionally fortunate or the exceptionally able, we need to envisage education as two stages in a single course which will embrace the whole development of childhood and adolescence up to sixteen, and obliterate the vulgar irrelevances of class inequality and economic pressure in a new educational synthesis.[16]

Four years later, in *Social Progress and Educational Waste*, Kenneth Lindsay asked:

> . . . how far the 'educational ladder' is effective; whether in fact it is, as it has been described, a greasy pole.
>
> Perhaps two figures will give perspective to the whole problem and point to the heart of the matter. First, of the 550,000 children who leave elementary schools each year, 9.5 per cent of an age group proceed to secondary schools, one-third exempt from fees and two-thirds paying, while 1 per 1,000 reach the university . . . at least 50 per cent of the pupils in elementary schools can profit by some form of post-primary education up to the age of 16 . . . Finally, it has been conclusively proved that success in winning scholarships varies with almost monotonous regularity according to the quality of the social and economic environment.[17]

The Hadow Committee of 1926, of which Tawney was an influential member, proposed an end to the elementary/secondary divide, and a redesignation of primary and secondary, with all pupils passing at about age 11 to secondary schools. This principle gained gradual acceptance, and its implementation was secured by the Education Act of 1944. Nevertheless, examination at age 11 still continued. Though all children would have access to secondary schools, they would not necessarily have access to the school they wished to attend. On average only some 20 per cent would be allotted to secondary grammar schools. The remainder would be consigned to secondary modern schools, with a few places in secondary technical schools. Such tripartism was justified on a variety of grounds, from Plato through Taunton to Norwood.

The Norwood Report of 1943 argued that there were three types of children (and presumably indeed of adults). Some were 'interested in learning for its own sake', of high intelligence, capable of abstract thought, suited to an academic curriculum and likely to succeed in rigorous external examinations. Such children, from whatever social background, should be given access to grammar schools from which they would proceed to white-collar jobs, the professions, and to the universities. Secondary technical schools were, as their name suggested, for those with 'an uncanny insight into the intricacies of mechanism'. Overall they catered for only some 4 per cent of secondary age children, and were not provided in many parts of the country. Thus the majority of children, those considered to be the future hewers of wood and drawers of water (in Norwood's terms those who 'deal more easily with concrete things rather than ideas') received their secondary schooling in institutions which were, in many ways, direct heirs to the elementary school tradition, both in terms of purpose and of status. Though parity of esteem between the three types of secondary schooling was supposed, it was never a reality. Secondary modern schools were financed less generously than grammar schools, and they attracted few graduate teachers. They made no, or very little, provision for children to continue their schooling beyond the statutory age. Between 1947 and 1972 pupils generally left secondary modern schools at age 15, while those in grammar schools continued to 16, or to 18.

Tripartism in English secondary schooling was not only based on the grounds that there were three types of children, but also reflected the belief that those three types of children could be accurately identified at age 11 by means of intelligence tests. In the inter-war years it was recognized that secondary schooling was historically inimical to large sections of the working class. Elementary schooling was the norm and many children had no chance of access to secondary schools, simply because they were not entered for the scholarship examination. Even those deemed to have a chance of securing a place were frequently deterred from applying by parents, teachers, or their own perceptions of the consequences of success. For secondary schooling involved a variety of costs, both real and hidden – for example uniforms and books, means-tested fees from 1931, the loss of potential earnings between the ages of 14 and 16, and possible alienation from family and friends.

After 1944 it was widely assumed that working-class access to grammar schools would substantially increase. Nevertheless, considerable variation in provision still existed. Some of this resulted from historic differences in provision and from population changes. Another major element, however, was the difference in wealth between local education authorities. In areas of considerable poverty and unemployment, revenue from rates yielded less money for educational purposes, including the building of grammar schools, than in more affluent neighbourhoods: thus access to secondary grammar schools depended to a considerable extent upon locality. In some areas 40 per cent of children might attend grammar schools, in others a mere 12 per cent. Accordingly there was no national standard for success in the examination: the percentage of passes depended upon the number of places available in a particular area.

Whilst variations in access on account of locality and provision might be plainly visible, the extent of other aspects of advantage and disadvantage was only revealed by pioneering studies from the 1950s and 1960s. For example, the concept of a basic intelligence quotient (IQ) which could be accurately measured for the purpose of selection for different types of secondary schools, was brought into question by studies which showed the beneficial effect of coaching upon IQ scores, in one instance an increase of sixteen points in an hour. English tests were subject to particular scrutiny. These, it was argued, provided not so much an examination of powers of reasoning and the potential for abstract thought, as an assessment of familial vocabulary, speech patterns and cultural norms. A further concern, given the criticisms of the concept of the doctrine of a basic intelligence quotient, was the practice of streaming in primary schools. While selection of children at 11 seemed in itself to be both inefficient and premature, research by Jackson[18] indicated that streaming in junior schools, with its effects upon the expectations of pupils, parents and teachers, often meant that crucial decisions about access to particular types of secondary schools were effectively being made from the age of 7.

In the post-war years concern mounted that access to grammar schools was still being determined by social class and region rather than by intelligence or ability. Though some dimensions of the relationship between social class and intelligence remained frustratingly elusive, Floud, Halsey and Martin's study of access to grammar schools in Middlesbrough and South West Hertfordshire showed that in the

1950s in these two areas the likelihood of a working-class boy gaining access to a grammar school differed little from what it had been some twenty years before. In 1953 only one working-class boy in eight in Middlesbrough and one in seven in South West Hertfordshire, gained access to a grammar school. The respective figures for sons of clerks were nearly one in three and one in two![19] Not only did children of working-class parents have considerably less access to secondary grammar schools than those of other social groups, once within the schools working-class children performed poorly in academic terms. An official report on early leaving, published in 1954, showed that of a sample group of 436 children of unskilled workers in grammar schools, 284 failed to secure three GCE 'O'-level passes. In sharp contrast, a survey in the 1960s of more than 1,000 public schoolboys who had failed the 11-plus examination revealed that some 70 per cent had achieved five or more passes at Ordinary level.[20] Thus working-class children were being denied access to secondary grammar schools by a selection system which militated against them in several ways. Even those who secured admission, however, were failing to gain access to sixth forms, universities and higher professional occupations in the same proportions as their more affluent contemporaries, both within maintained and independent schools.

Although selection at 11-plus was not necessarily final (in some local education authorities pupils from secondary modern schools might transfer to technical or grammar school during their courses, and others at ages 15 or 16) growing concerns about the unreliability and inefficiency of selection, and the loss of talent which it entailed, led to the comprehensive secondary school movement. Reform began in such rural areas as the Isle of Man and Windermere. Kidbrooke, the first purpose-built comprehensive school in London, opened its doors in 1954. In one sense the movement was a considerable success: by the 1980s over 90 per cent of children of secondary age in the maintained sector attended secondary schools designated as comprehensive. On the other hand many of the aspirations of the proponents of comprehensive schools were not realized. Some grammar schools remained, effectively ensuring that comprehensive schools in their areas retained many features of secondary modern status. Comprehensive schools still reflected wide variations in academic opportunities, resources and achievements. The abilities of such schools to compensate for family and other disadvantages and to promote a more egalitarian society were severely tried. Some argued, indeed, that bright working-class children in deprived areas were disadvantaged by the change, finding themselves in 'sink' schools rather than having the opportunity to escape from their surroundings via the traditional grammar school route. Other explanations for the failure of secondary comprehensive schools adequately to fulfil all the expectations of their supporters centred upon the survival of such practices as streaming, the reluctance to develop an adequate range of curricula and assessment techniques, and the continuing influence of family and home circumstances – poverty, single-parenthood, low expectations, lack of homework facilities.

Although the rigid class divisions of nineteenth-century England were modified to some extent in the twentieth century, and there was no crop of prestigious new educational foundations of the public school type, independent schools continued to flourish. This has ensured that access to the most powerful and influential schools in England has been largely reserved to children of the wealthy. One recurrent difficulty in terms of access has been the continuing difference between age of transfer – 11 in maintained schools, 13 in independent. Nevertheless, some independent schools have long reserved a few scholarship places for very able children from any background, while a minority of schools have managed to bestride the independent and maintained traditions. For example, from 1919 some grammar schools received direct grants from the government, and from 1944 were required to provide a minimum of 25 per cent of free places for children from local authority primary schools. In the 1970s the abolition of direct grant status led to the majority of these 178 schools moving fully into the independent sector. The assisted places scheme of 1980 provided a new bridge between maintained primary and independent secondary schools. More radical schemes to provide access to such schools – from the Left by removal of charitable status or complete integration into the maintained system, from the Right by means of a voucher system – have been posited, but not yet attempted.

Access to higher education has also depended largely upon the twin features of extent of provision and financial support. To remain in full-time education beyond the age of 18, and possibly even until 21 or 22, was a luxury which very few could afford. In consequence provision was limited, and access closely circumscribed. For some six centuries there were but two effective universities in England, those of Oxford and Cambridge. Access to these institutions, in terms of student numbers as a percentage of the total population, peaked in the 1630s, but by the middle of the nineteenth century they still bore the reputation of professional schools for the Anglican clergy and finishing establishments for the sons of the wealthy. In contrast London University, which dates from the 1830s, and the university foundations of the second half of the nineteenth century in such cities as Birmingham, Manchester and Leeds, were attended by many students from the lower-middle and artisan classes, with considerable numbers engaged in non-degree studies and part-time attendance. From 1902 the new local education authorities were empowered to give scholarships to university students, and from 1919 some 200 state scholarships were made available annually for students from grant aided secondary schools. Nevertheless, higher education in England was for an elite, and remained so even after 1962 when local education authorities were obliged to give a grant, albeit on a means-tested scale, to any suitably qualified student who gained an undergraduate university place. The Robbins Report of 1963 indicated the need both for a further expansion of places in higher education, and for greater access for members of the working classes. The Robbins principle was that access to higher education should be provided for all who had the requisite ability. It noted that 'the proportion of middle-class children who reach degree level courses is eight times as high as the proportion from working-class homes'.[21]

Though, until the second half of the twentieth century, access to universities was restricted, in the last 200 years there has been a rich variety of higher or adult education institutions that have catered for broad strata of the population. The nineteenth century saw the formation of mechanics' institutes, Owenite and Chartist halls, mutual improvement societies, university extension courses, polytechnics and the provision of many free and subscription libraries. In the early years of the twentieth century these were complemented by the Workers' Educational Association, the development of university extra-mural activities, and a variety of provision at local education authority level. From 1971 the Open University, with its range of study methods – radio and television programmes, correspondence work, written assignments, tutorials and summer schools – gave access to higher education to a much wider group of students, both in terms of social class and of age. It soon became the largest university in the land.

Gender

The term 'gender' is used here to refer to the several social and cultural differences between males and females.

For most of English history males and females were accorded different roles and status. As a result they also had access to different types of education. In broad terms, it can be stated that males monopolized political, economic, professional and religious positions, and that females were denied access to such fields, and to the educational systems which led to them. For example, until the twentieth century women could not be Members of Parliament, judges or priests. Accordingly, they were generally denied access to grammar schools, and excluded from universities. They were also barred from such areas of professional training as the Inns of Court. There were some exceptions, for example female monarchs such as Elizabeth in the sixteenth century and Victoria in the nineteenth, who wielded considerable influence. Even these examples, however, may be seen as the exercise of familial, rather than female, power.

An understanding of the historic nature and extent of male power within English society is central to an understanding of the issue of gender and education. When, in the second half of the nineteenth century, women gained legal access to some educational institutions from which they had previously been excluded, for example the Universities of Oxford and Cambridge, such access, though highly important in an individual and symbolic sense, would do little to effect change in the gender power relationships in society more broadly. As the figures in the introduction to this chapter indicate, more than one hundred years later women's access to senior professional positions, not least in the very Universities of Oxford and Cambridge themselves, still appears to be severely limited.

Access to basic education for both boys and girls has been a constant feature in English history. Girls, like boys, would need to learn the basic rudiments of speech and manners, of religious observance and social custom. The vocational skills necessary for boys would be acquired from their fathers, or through employment. Similarly, girls would learn domestic duties and skills, appropriate both for the roles of servant and housewife, from their mothers, and in the domestic environment. Where children attended parish or charity schools, all would be given a basic religious education, and would normally be taught to read. Writing and arithmetic were subjects sometimes deemed to be more appropriate for boys than for girls. During the nineteenth century boys and girls attended elementary schools in substantially the same numbers, and in 1880 such schooling was made compulsory. Nevertheless attendance patterns and length of schooling of boys and girls might differ considerably, according to the exigencies of family circumstances or the attractions of local employment. In terms of curriculum, whilst the basic subjects of religion and the three Rs might be common, girls were frequently denied access to other academic subjects by the time they were required to spend upon such subjects as needlework and domestic economy. The most important restriction on access, however, related to a hidden curriculum whereby boys and girls were strenuously schooled into gender-specific values and attitudes.

In the nineteenth century boys and girls of the middle and upper classes also had access to education in basic skills and duties. Such teaching would have taken place in a domestic context, at the hands of parent, governess or tutor. For boys, however, it would be necessary to make their way in a public sphere and as providers for the family. Male occupations in such areas as politics, law, Church, medicine, army, navy, agriculture, industry and commerce, would require access to education which could rarely be supplied within the family. Girls, on the other hand, had little or no access to such public worlds, and hence to the educational institutions – public and grammar schools, universities and professional bodies – from which they were supplied. The schools they attended were private, rather than public, establishments, in which they acquired domestic and social skills. While boys and girls of a particular family might be taught together at home in their early years, one of the most distinctive features of the schools (day and boarding) which existed for children of these classes was that they were either for boys or for girls. Access by members of the opposite sex was strictly denied.

Accordingly, in the second half of the nineteenth century schools for girls arose which exhibited fewer domestic features, and bore more resemblance to the grammar and public schools attended by boys. The high schools of the Girls' Public Day School Company, modelled on the North London Collegiate School founded by Frances Buss, were essentially day schools of a grammar school type. Prestigious boarding schools for girls, more akin to the boys' public schools, included Cheltenham Ladies' College, Roedean and Wycombe Abbey. Such schools, however, were very few in number. Access, therefore, remained limited. Although these schools provided a more rigorous academic curriculum and some of their pupils proceeded to further study at university level, they did not constitute any substantial challenge to male domination of the public sphere. While the field of education itself might supply important new opportunities for professional employment, in general for the well-educated, as for the poorly-educated woman, marriage remained the main career.

The report of the Taunton Commission was one important landmark in improving girls' access to secondary schooling, several existing endowments being subsequently reorganized to provide for girls' as well as boys' grammar schools. The Education Act of 1902 was another. Now local education authorities were empowered to establish their own secondary schools. Given the existence of traditional grammar schools for boys, the majority of new foundations were for girls. The tradition of single-sex schooling at secondary level thus continued, until the advent of comprehensive reform. Twenty years ago there were nearly 2,000 maintained girls' schools in England; in 1994 there were fewer than 250. Yet league tables of examination results suggest that independent schools for girls continue to be both popular and successful. The Education Act of 1944 gave universal access to secondary education, and fifty years later the achievements of girls in GCSE and GCE 'A'-level examinations surpassed those of boys.

CONCLUSION

Five conclusions may be drawn from the application of historical perspectives to current discussion of issues of access in education.

The first is that access both to self-directed and formally-provided education is greater than ever before. In the last fifty years a general rise in the standard of living, coupled with unprecedented technological advances – radios, televisions, video recorders, computers – has revolutionized the potential for personal access to education, both informal and formal. Over the last 200 years there has been an undeniable increase in the provision of formal educational facilities. Even within the last ten years an expansion of institutions of further and higher education, coupled with a decline in juvenile employment and in the numbers of unskilled jobs, has substantially increased participation rates in full-time education beyond the ages of 16 and 18. Increased participation has regularly prompted expressions of concern that 'more means worse', in the sense that greater access leads to a decline in the standards of qualifications. But such concerns, however justifiable, must be balanced by the clear evidence that each widening of access, as for example in 1944 or 1963, has shown that many of those who would previously have been excluded from secondary or higher education could, by their participation, benefit both themselves and society more broadly.

It is also apparent that many historic restrictions in respect of the access of certain groups to formal education have been relaxed. Although single-sex schools and others dedicated to pupils of particular religious creeds still exist, in general, educational inequalities based on such grounds as sex and faith have been removed.

The second conclusion is that trends towards enlarged access are neither universal nor irreversible. For example during the middle ages, when Roman Catholicism was the church of England, many poor boys had access to education to ensure a continuous supply of celibate clergy. Even after the sixteenth-century Reformation many grammar schools educated boys from a wider social spectrum than did those of the late-nineteenth century. During the nineteenth century in some areas of the country opportunities for access to institutions of formal education declined as the school population outran the means of supply. Another key factor which reduced access at particular points in the twentieth century (as in the nineteenth) was economic depression, particularly when accompanied by adult unemployment. It might also be argued that although the communications revolution of the last fifty years has great educational potential, the use of the media, both old and new, for commercial and entertainment purposes has diminished rather than increased actual participation in worthwhile activities. At the same time there has been a reduction in access to what might be called moral education. Though morality is not necessarily dependent upon religion, one symptom of this change is that educational agencies such as churches and Sunday schools have declined in numbers and influence.

A third conclusion emphasises that historical perspectives change. For example, most historical writing about gender and access has, understandably, emphasised the nature and extent of female exclusion from worthwhile education. In 1996 the emphasis is reversed. Why are boys performing less well than girls? Why do they supply such a large proportion of the criminal population? To what extent have schools, and education more broadly, contributed towards an anti-intellectual culture amongst English males of all classes? Why have boys for so long been excluded from a curriculum that would have supplied them with basic domestic skills, thus rendering them dependent upon females?

A fourth concerns the relationship between education and society. It is commonly argued, and with some justification, that education cannot of itself change society. Historical perspectives confirm that in terms of access (and of achievement) the influence of social class and family may well outweigh that of school. Not only is upward social mobility difficult in English society, it also true that those in power, understandably are reluctant to cede or share such power with others with superior educational achievement. Even when girls outperform boys in schools other factors restrict their access to positions of power and authority.

This relationship between society and education finds expression in concepts of schooling. For centuries the concept of parish, charity and elementary schooling was that of providing a basic literacy and of preparing the children of the poor to live contentedly in the station to which it had pleased God to call them, in the hope of a life hereafter. By the beginning of the twentieth century the restrictive and demeaning dimensions of such a concept were widely condemned. Since the sixteenth century the basic concept of secondary schooling in England has been that of the grammar school. By the third quarter of the twentieth century that tradition, with its connotations of rural classicism and clericalism, selection and scholasticism, was, in its turn, seen as restrictive by those who believed that secondary education for all required the provision of a much broader range of curricula and institutions for those in the 11 to 18 age range.

Finally, the historical perspective provides insight into current debates about access, debates which reflect the continued existence of two competing models which have deep historical roots. The first model may broadly be described as a common school for a common culture. Its origins may be traced back at least as far as the philosophical, religious and political radicals of the late eighteenth and early nineteenth centuries. These reformers wanted to increase the role of the state in education as a means of diminishing the power of established and endowed bodies, notably the Anglican Church, public schools and universities. They no doubt would have welcomed a national curriculum if it were to provide an educational entitlement for all. Their twentieth-century successors, the trade unions, the Labour Party and certain local education authorities, have been curiously irresolute in promoting this model, as the example of the secondary comprehensive school shows. Since 1979 the exclusion of such groups from political power has meant that changes in educational access have taken place within a more differentiated, rather than a more common, social structure.

The second model is that which accepts the existence of natural hierarchies in schools as in society at large. Modern state intervention in education in England which began in the nineteenth century, though it was called national education, did not promote the concept of a common school for a common culture. National education was envisaged and applied by the state as a means of providing some schooling for those who could not help themselves, or whose choices of schools were considered to be unwise. Throughout the nineteenth and twentieth centuries many of those who presided over state education in England identified it essentially as education for the poor, for those who, unlike themselves, could not or would not pay for the schooling of their own children. One of their key purposes, therefore, was to ensure that the education of the poor did not challenge the education of the wealthy. In contrast to many other European countries whose social hierarchies were severely weakened or overthrown during revolution and war, and who used education as part of the process of building or rebuilding their states, in England the most prestigious educational institutions, the Universities of Oxford and Cambridge, and the boys' public schools, still reflect the middle- and upper-class male domination of such institutions during the middle years of the nineteenth century.

NOTES

1. *Sunday Times*, 23 February 1992.
2. *The Times*, 7 November 1994; 10 November 1994.
3. *The Times*, 10 November 1994.
4. *The Times*, 1 May 1995.
5. *National Commission Report*, 1993, 9–10.
6. OFSTED, 1993.
7. *The Times*, 1 November 1993.
8. Simon, 1994, 179.
9. *The Times*, 16 November 1994.
10. *National Commission Report*, 1993, 160–1.
11. *Guardian*, 18 November 1993.
12. Gillian Shephard quoted in *The Times*, 10 November 1994.
13. John, 1992, 140–1.
14. Quoted in Sutherland, 1971, 24.
15. Quoted in Maclure, 1969, 87–8.
16. Quoted in Silver, 1973, 8.
17. Quoted in Silver, 1973, 28–9.
18. Jackson, 1964.
19. Quoted in Silver, 1973, 163.
20. Aldrich, 1982, 121.
21. Quoted in Silver, 1973, 204.

SUGGESTED READING

Arnot, M. (1985) *Race and Gender: Equal Opportunities Policies in Education.*

Dyhouse, C. (1981) *Girls Growing Up in Late Victorian and Edwardian England.*

Hunt, F. (1991) *Gender and Policy in English Education: Schooling for Girls 1902–1944.*

Rattansi, A. and Reeder, D. (eds) (1992) *Rethinking Radical Education: Essays in Honour of Brian Simon.*

Sanderson, M. (1987) *Educational Opportunity and Social Change in England.*

Silver, H. (ed.) (1973) *Equal Opportunity in Education.*

Stone, M. (1985) *The Education of the Black Child: the Myth of Multiracial Education.*

TWO

Curriculum

CURRENT ISSUES

The term 'curriculum' is used in two ways. In the narrow sense it means the formal courses and classes offered by an educational institution. The broader definition embraces all the learning experiences that take place in an educational institution or elsewhere, including those elements sometimes described as 'extra-curricular' or the 'hidden curriculum'.

Three broad classifications of curricula may be established at this point: child- or person-centred, subject-based and vocational. The three types may co-exist in the one educational institution, may be characteristic of different types of educational institutions, or may be identified with certain stages in an individual's education. For example, education may be predominantly child-centred in nursery and infant schools; subject-based during the years of compulsory schooling under the National Curriculum; and vocational preparation for general or particular types of employment in the concluding stages of formal education.

Since 1979, government education policies have promoted two of these three broad curricular classifications at the expense of the third. Vocationally directed curricular reforms have proliferated: for example, the Certificate of Pre-Vocational Education (CPVE), the Technical and Vocational Education Initiative (TVEI), National Vocational Qualifications (NVQs). The National Curriculum of 1988 was subject-based. Child-centred education, on the other hand, has found less favour, indeed has been cited as a major cause of low expectations and underachievement in English schools. Some critics of government curriculum policy, however, have argued that the continuing separation between vocational and subject-based, and the very traditional nature of National Curriculum subjects, constitute the major curriculum problems of today. Other critics, both from the Left and Right of the political spectrum, have questioned why a government devoted to choice and diversity has not applied such principles to the school curriculum.

Denis Lawton has suggested that a school curriculum may be understood as a selection of knowledge, values and attitudes from a society's culture which it is considered important to transmit to the next generation.[1] This is a useful starting point, but it must be complemented by two other insights. The first is that a curriculum is not just a matter of content, but also of control. Who is to make the selection? The second, that the school curriculum may become a means of challenging, rather than transmitting, certain elements of the knowledge, values and attitudes of a society. For a curriculum does not simply represent a selection from the culture of a society as it was or is, it may also reflect a vision, or visions, of what that society should be in the future. Thus a curriculum may become an area of contest between those who wish to preserve, and those who wish to change, certain features of society. For example, in a hierarchical and patriarchal society different curricula may be supplied for different groups in that society, with such differences being justified in terms of expectations and roles based upon social class and sex. Reformers may advocate a common curriculum for all, irrespective of class or sex, as a means of diminishing such hierarchical and patriarchal features, and of transforming expectations and roles.

Societies and their cultures change over time. For example, an imperial power may lose its empire, and therefore no longer require its traditional ruling caste and the curriculum which produced it. Similarly, there may be little point in producing a working class of uneducated hewers of wood and drawers of water, if all citizens need a high degree of knowledge and skills to function efficiently in a modern society, and manual jobs are fast disappearing. On the other hand, even in a truly democratic society, while all may have an entitlement of access to the full curricular range, in practice some elements of curriculum may, on grounds of interest, ability or future role, be meaningful only to a small number of students.

One recent example of contest and challenge which reflected differing visions of the past and future of English society, its culture, knowledge, values and attitudes, was the often heated debate about what should be taught in history lessons under the new National Curriculum. The architect of the 1988 Act, Kenneth Baker, in common with Margaret Thatcher, wanted history lessons to focus upon British history and to reflect Britain's past achievements and glories: 'Our pride in our past', he declared, 'enables us to walk tall in the world today.'[2] Others, however, while acknowledging the importance of citizenship education, maintained that a less celebratory approach to the past, for example one which gave greater prominence to the histories and rights of other nations, and even to examples of British misdeeds, would be a salutary and long-overdue corrective.

Current curriculum issues have found a focus in the National Curriculum of 1988. That curriculum was designed to ensure that pupils of compulsory school age in maintained schools followed a ten-subject course with English, mathematics and science at the core, and history, geography, technology, a modern foreign language (from age 11), art, music and physical education as foundation subjects. Statutory orders laid down 'programmes of study' and 'attainment targets' for each subject. Programmes of study constitute the knowledge, skills and understanding which pupils are expected to follow in the four stages of schooling: Key Stage One (age 5–7), Two (7–11), Three (11–14) and Four (14–16).

Difficulties since 1988, including opposition from the teaching profession to certain aspects of the curriculum and its accompanying programmes of testing, prompted the government to invite Sir Ron Dearing, chairman-designate of the School Curriculum and Assessment Authority (SCAA), 'to review the manageability of the National Curriculum and the testing system'. The main conclusions and recommendations of this review, published in 1994, were as follows:

> The National Curriculum is fundamental to raising educational standards. Urgent action is needed to reduce the statutorily required content of its programmes of study and to make it less prescriptive and less complex. A closely co-ordinated review of all statutory curriculum Orders should immediately be put in hand, guided by the need to:
> i   reduce the volume of material required by law to be taught;
> ii simplify and clarify the programmes of study;
> iii reduce prescription so as to give more scope for professional judgement;
> iv ensure that the Orders are written in a way which offers maximum support to the classroom teacher.[3]

These changes, which the government agreed to implement, went some way towards meeting one of the major criticisms of the original National Curriculum – that it was unmanageable. Nevertheless a number of criticisms still remain and these lie at the heart of current debate.

- It is not truly national. It does not apply nationally across the whole of the United Kingdom, and even in England and Wales it does not apply to independent schools.
- It is still too substantial and prescriptive and takes up too much time.
- It is based upon subjects. A truly national curriculum should encompass vocational and person-centred dimensions. SCAA should be merged with the National Council for Vocational Qualifications (NCVQ).
- It is still too closely controlled by central government.
- It is tied too closely to assessment. This means that there will be 'teaching to the test' and other curriculum areas will be neglected.
- It should be sensitive to the needs of older pupils. Either Key Stage Four should make provision for the 14–18 age range, or a separate Key Stage Five should be established.

HISTORICAL PERSPECTIVES

Medieval and early modern

In the medieval period education was essentially social, religious and vocational. Parents, priests and employers determined what was studied, and how. There was a strong oral tradition and such basic Christian tenets as the Lord's Prayer, creed, and ten commandments could all be learned by heart. By the fourteenth century however, a standardized alphabet had emerged, written English was widely used, and parish, song, reading and writing schools were all in evidence. The purpose of such schools was to provide certain elements of instruction in a more efficient manner than could be supplied elsewhere. The term 'curriculum', as applied to schools, meant the course that had to be run or undertaken there.

Royal injunctions and foundation statutes provide some evidence as to curriculum content and practice at this time, but the nature and extent of such changes as occurred are difficult to determine. No doubt the Protestant Reformation of the sixteenth century gave a boost to reading as a means of acquiring a fuller understanding of the Bible and prayer book. By the eighteenth century, although there were working and workhouse schools which placed considerable emphasis upon a vocational curriculum, parish and charity schools were still providing a basic diet of Christianity and reading. Writing and arithmetic were taught more frequently to boys as a means of preparation for apprenticeship or employment; girls spent more time on domestic pursuits, particularly needlework. Though most charity schools catered for day pupils, some were residential and provided board, lodging and clothes for their orphaned and outcast clientele. Sunday schools, which grew rapidly from the 1780s, provided a new emphasis upon the religious dimensions of the curriculum.

Vocational education might take place within the family or household, but a variety of specialist locations also existed. The system of craft apprenticeship required boys, and less frequently girls, to be bound for a period of some seven years during which time they not only learned the mysteries of their craft, but also acquired a range of other social and educational skills. Similarly, boys and girls who were dedicated at an early age to life in a monastery or convent were required to submit to the rules and training of their orders.

The most distinctive element in the medieval curriculum, and one which was to have a profound effect over several centuries, was Latin. Medieval grammar schools were founded essentially to teach the Latin language, the international language of the Church, the law and of scholarship. Although some grammar schools also taught song, reading and writing, and others Greek, and although grammar school foundations of the eighteenth century showed a renewed concern for the teaching of 'English' subjects, Latin, its reading, writing and speaking, was the prime concern. Founders' statutes sometimes provided that only Latin, or occasionally Latin or Greek, should be spoken in school. Teaching was from classic texts. The *Ars Minor* (c. 350) of Aelius Donatus was so widely used during the medieval period that grammar school pupils were sometimes referred to as 'donats' or 'donatists'. Given the shortage of books, much recourse was still made to oral methods, while some textbooks were written in verse. One of these, the *Doctrinale* of Alexander de Villa Dei of Brittany, which consisted of some 2,650 hexameters, was so widely used that it went through more than 250 editions between 1470 and the 1520s. The Reformation saw an important intervention by central government in respect of the grammar school curriculum. In 1540 Henry VIII, by royal proclamation, decreed that only one Latin grammar should be used in schools, that originally compiled by Erasmus, and John Colet and William Lily, respectively founder and first high master of St Paul's School. In 1758 this *Royal Grammar* was transmuted into the *Eton Latin Grammar*, and remained the standard work until the second half of the nineteenth century.

During the eighteenth century there was a decline in the demand for Latin. Some grammar schools, including those which developed into public schools in the nineteenth century, continued to concentrate upon the classics and to send boys to universities; others broadened their curricula in response to local needs. For example, some grammar schools in coastal towns added such subjects as arithmetic, astronomy, book-keeping, geography, geometry, merchants' accounts, modern foreign languages, natural philosophy and writing. Other grammar schools reverted to elementary subjects only.

Studies in the medieval universities of Oxford and Cambridge were derived from the seven liberal arts, the *trivium* of grammar, logic and rhetoric, and the *quadrivium* of arithmetic, astronomy, geometry and music. In addition to the basic arts course there were higher faculties of theology, medicine, canon law and civil law. All teaching and study was in Latin. Legal training also took place in London, in the four Inns of Court and the ten Chancery inns. Scholastic philosophy and the classics continued to dominate the university curriculum until the end of the eighteenth century. Mathematics became firmly established within the arts course at Cambridge, particularly after the publication of Isaac Newton's *Principia Mathematica* in 1687, but the universities were not generally at the forefront of new learning, nor did they develop as professional schools, except for the training of Anglican clergy. Their purpose was to promote godly and traditional learning, to train the intellect, and also to act as finishing schools for the sons of the wealthy. Curriculum development at this tertiary level was to be found rather in the Dissenting Academies, for example that founded by Philip Doddridge at Northampton, or the Warrington Academy where Joseph Priestley, himself a product of the Northampton Academy during its removal to Daventry, taught in the 1760s. The academies combined traditional and modern subjects. Evidence relating to 196 of the students at Warrington Academy in the second half of the eighteenth century shows that ninety-eight were entered for Commerce, fifty-two for Divinity, twenty-four for Medicine and twenty-two for Law.[4]

Nineteenth century

During the nineteenth century new forces arose to shape society, educational provision and the curriculum. England was transformed by rapid population growth, industrialization, urbanization and imperialism, and by a communications revolution which encompassed both the application of steam power to land and water transport, and cheap postage and popular newspapers. These changes also had a profound effect upon the nature and role of the state, and upon its role in respect of the school curriculum.

Elementary schools of the nineteenth century, including those promoted by the Anglican National and non-denominational British societies, continued the charity school curriculum of religious instruction together with reading, writing and arithmetic. In the early years of the century the widespread use of the monitorial, or mutual, system, whereby older pupils were used to instruct the younger, probably reinforced the drill element in the teaching and learning process. The pupil teacher system, begun in 1846, however, required these teaching apprentices to study arithmetic, English grammar and composition, geography, history, religious knowledge, vocal music, and school method and organization. Additionally, boys were to learn algebra, mechanics, mensuration and surveying, and girls, needlework. It is not clear to what extent this potential for a broader curriculum was implemented in elementary schools of the time. Though statistics from this period must always be viewed with considerable caution, the Education Census of 1851 reported that of the elementary schools of England and Wales 98 per cent taught reading, but only 68 per cent writing and 61 per cent arithmetic. Industrial occupations were taught by a mere 2 per cent. Ten years later, the report of the Newcastle Commission, nevertheless, regretted that teachers were spending too much time on older pupils, and possibly on the more esoteric studies, and concluded that the basic subjects, and younger pupils, were being neglected.

Back (or forward) to basics was the thrust of the Revised Code of 1862. Henceforth a considerable part of the government grant to assisted elementary schools would be given according to the achievements of pupils in the three Rs – reading, writing and arithmetic. The Revised Code, with its principle of payment by results, represented a substantial intervention by government in curriculum matters, an intervention which weakened not only the power of school parents, teachers and managers in this regard, but also marked a notable shift from a religious to a secular curriculum. The Christian ethos still survived and religion was still taught, though not in some of the board schools established from 1870, but secular subjects were now centre stage. Exercises in reading and writing were prescribed in secular rather than divine texts – 'a short ordinary paragraph in a newspaper, or other modern narrative'.

Although the influence of teachers and parents upon the curricula of private working-class schools, attended by more than half a million pupils in 1858, remained paramount, in the second half of the nineteenth century the numbers of such schools rapidly declined. Gradually the government used its financial power to extend the elementary school curriculum. From 1867 a new range of grants was introduced. These were known as 'specific' subjects, unlike the 'class' subjects whereby grants were given on the proficiency demonstrated by the class as a whole, rather than by individuals. The list of specific and class subjects eventually included botany, English literature, geography, grammar, history, mathematics, mechanics, and even French and German. Not all elementary schools offered one or more of such subjects: much depended upon the capacity of the school managers to provide the necessary teachers and equipment.

The large school boards, as in London or Birmingham, were to the fore in curriculum innovation. Manual training, physical education and music, for example, featured in many London board schools. In the 1890s increasing concern about foreign industrial competition led to a shift towards such subjects as book-keeping, drawing, manual instruction and shorthand. The system of payment by results was relaxed, and in 1895 the annual examination of older pupils was abolished. In the later decades of the nineteenth century more emphasis came to be placed on extra-curricular dimensions, when school boards and other agencies began to attend to the social needs of their children, with the provision of cheap or free dinners, articles of clothing, evening associations and clubs.

The curriculum of the nineteenth-century elementary school represented a very particular selection from Victorian culture. Pupils were schooled to be citizens and workers in a general rather than a specific sense. They were taught to know their duty to God and to their betters, and how to recognize and defer to the latter. They were provided with a basic literacy and numeracy and, in the case of girls, such domestic skills as would enable them to be useful servants, and subsequently good wives and mothers. The curriculum of the elementary school, like the elementary school itself, was an end in itself: it was not generally intended to be preparatory to further studies. Towards the end of the century, however, some elementary schools, for example the famous Fleet Road Board School, in London's Hampstead, did indeed prepare pupils for entry to grammar schools.

Just as the examination system originally prescribed under the Revised Code of 1862 was a prime means of standardizing curricula in the elementary school, so examinations had a significant influence on the curricula of other establishments, including the grammar schools and universities. Examinations and other issues of assessment will be considered in detail in the next chapter, but one important point about nineteenth-century examinations must be noted here. While examinations under the Revised Code, and those conducted under the auspices of the Science and Art Department established at South Kensington after the Great Exhibition of 1851, were under direct government control, other examinations were not. They proceeded from such bodies as the College of Preceptors, an independent body of schoolteachers, or from the universities. In curriculum and in examinations, as in other matters of schooling, government intervention was reluctant, and mainly for the purpose of helping those whom it was widely believed could not, or should not, be allowed to help themselves. In 1867 Robert Lowe, architect of the Revised Code, declared that:

> I do not think it is any part of the duty of Government to prescribe what people should learn, except in the case of the poor, where time is so limited that we must fix upon a few elementary subjects to get anything done at all. I think it is the duty of the parents to fix what their children should learn.[5]

Indeed, on occasion government intervention was for the purpose of providing greater freedom in curriculum matters. The Grammar School Act of 1840 allowed grammar schools to depart from the terms of their founding statutes and to diversify the curriculum by the addition of such subjects as English language and literature, mathematics, modern languages, and modern geography and history. Even prior to this legislation, however, although classical study still occupied a central place in the education of boys of the professional and upper classes, the existence of public, grammar and private schools, academies of various types, tutors and the continuing tradition of the Grand Tour, meant that there was considerable variety both in curricular provision and practice.

Curricula for girls of the middling or upper classes were subject to even less central control. Girls from such sectors of society were educated either at home by parents or governesses, or in private day or boarding schools. Curricula were determined by providers and purchasers. There were no foundation statutes or other regulations, and classical studies could be included or excluded as seemed appropriate. Nevertheless, though infinite variety might prevail, instruction in spiritual and moral values, social skills such as etiquette and deportment, in reading, writing, music, drawing, French and other accomplishments lay at the heart of the curriculum provided for such girls.

The Clarendon Commission of 1864, which reported on the nine great public schools for boys, recommended that although room should be found for such subjects as mathematics, modern languages and natural science, pride of place should continue to go to the classics. Teaching in such schools and at the universities was no longer in Latin, nor was it the language of the established church, but Latin, and to a lesser extent Greek, still constituted a common core. Rationalizations now centred upon the antiquity of these subjects, their difficulty, their capacity for mental training, their importance for the learning of other languages, their concerns with grammatical accuracy, their worth as a source of moral and cultural values. Above all classics provided males of the upper and middling classes with a badge, a means of distinction and expression, which would be unintelligible to those who had not received such an education.

The only real challenge to classics, a challenge which arose in the second half of the nineteenth century, was that of the games cult. At the beginning of the nineteenth century it was sufficient for the headmaster of a prestigious boys' public or grammar school to be in holy orders and a renowned classicist. By the end of the century it was also helpful to have a reputation on the cricket field. Some schools which had particular connections with the Empire, for example Haileybury or Cheltenham, did make provision for such exotic and esoteric subjects as Hindustani and Sanskrit. In general, however, English boys acquired their confidence to direct, whether at home or in the colonies, the largest Empire the world had ever seen, by a threefold initiation process. First, boys were separated from their families at an early age and placed in rurally located boarding schools. There they were schooled by physical hardship and punishment, and by a curriculum based essentially upon Christianity, classics and organized sport. The concept of an English gentleman drew, selectively, upon the glory that was Greece and the grandeur that was Rome, upon the moral and spiritual supremacy of Christianity over other faiths, and upon the creation and achievements of the games cult. Finally, equipped with the outward symbols of this curriculum – the public school accent, the old school tie, the ability to introduce classical allusions at appropriate points, whether in Parliament or the Punjab, and to be a sport – the English gentleman sallied forth into the world. Both the concept, and the curriculum which produced it, were to continue until well into the twentieth century.

The course of studies followed in nineteenth-century boys' public schools was not so very different from that in some grammar schools. It was the broader curriculum, based upon a combination of ancient foundations, boarding, substantial buildings and playing fields, the social origins of boys and masters, connections with the ancient universities, and with the public and professional worlds, that constituted a unique selection from the nation's culture. Proficiency in subjects not contained within that curriculum – applied science, technology, commerce – was not only regarded as being of little worth, it was also a mark of not being a gentleman. Concern about the low esteem afforded to science and technology in many, though not all secondary schools, was voiced on many occasions. For example, in the 1870s the reports of the Devonshire Commission showed that of 128 endowed schools from which returns had been received, more than half taught no science at all, while only thirteen had a laboratory. The Commissioners wished to place science on the same footing as language and mathematics, and to deny a degree to any person who had not demonstrated a fundamental level of scientific attainment. They stressed the need for more science teachers in secondary schools, and for science to form a more substantial part of the curriculum of training colleges and elementary schools. The sixth report of the Commission, published in 1875, concluded that:

> We are compelled, therefore, to record our opinion that the present state of scientific instruction in our schools is extremely unsatisfactory. The omission from a liberal education of a great branch of intellectual culture is of itself a matter for serious regret; and, considering the increasing importance of Science to the material interests of the country, we cannot but regard its almost total exclusion from the training of the upper and middle classes as little less than a national misfortune.[6]

It also spelled out a challenge to Latin:

> But the true teaching of Science consists, not merely in imparting the facts of Science, but in habituating the pupil to observe for himself, to reason for himself on what he observes, and to check the conclusions at which he arrives by further observation or experiment. And it may well be doubted whether, in this point of view, any other educational study offers the same advantage for developing and training the mental faculties by means of a great variety of appropriate exercises.[7]

One member of the Commission, Thomas Henry Huxley, regretted the omission of scientific studies both from elementary and secondary schools. Rather were such studies to be found in a 'nocturnal and somewhat surreptitious, position', in evening classes supported by grants from the Science and Art Department. Huxley concluded that an anti-scientific culture, represented in the upper classes and at governmental level, prevailed in England. He gave evidence that the division between the work of the Education Department and the Department of Science and Art, thus 'separating the teaching of science from education, is like cutting education in half', and 'an anomaly which could only exist in our own country'.[8]

The Samuelson Commission, which inquired into technical education in the 1880s, painted a similarly disturbing picture. It called for more scientific and technical studies in elementary and secondary schools, and in the training colleges. The Technical Instruction Act of 1889 did allow the new County and County Boroughs, established in the previous year, to spend the equivalent of a penny rate, and from

1890 the so-called 'Whisky money' (raised from a tax on alcoholic beverages) on the promotion of scientific and technical education. Indeed, the last decades of the nineteenth century, both in respect of university, polytechnic and other forms of adult education, appeared to promise a substantial broadening of the curriculum.

Twentieth century

By 1900 the categories of compulsory, specific and class, devised for the purposes of payment by results were abolished. In their place was a list of subjects expected to be taught 'as a rule'. Elementary school pupils were expected to study English, arithmetic, geography, history, physical exercises, drawing for boys and needlework for girls, together with one or more from a list of other subjects which could be taken if approved by the Inspector. The 1904 Code may be interpreted in two ways. It was couched in broad terms – 'form and strengthen the character', develop 'habits of observation and clear reasoning' and give 'some power over language' – and recognized the need to identify individual pupils of exceptional ability who should be prepared to continue their education in secondary schools. It may also be seen as a precursor to the *Handbook of Suggestions for Teachers*, published at regular intervals from 1905, whose very title seemed to acknowledge that in matters of curriculum and of teaching methods, teachers themselves should have the final say. On the other hand, given that most elementary school pupils did not proceed to secondary education and that compulsory schooling ended at age 12, such phrases as 'some power', and 'make the best use of the school years available', were a tacit admittance that an elementary (in every sense of the word) curriculum, with elementary standards of attainment, was intended and expected.

The Hadow Report of 1926 proposed the ending of the elementary school and a reorganization of education into two stages – primary and secondary. The Hadow Report of 1931, which examined courses of study suitable for children aged between 7 and 11 years, identified three phases in the curriculum history of the past hundred years. The first period, it maintained, was characterized by a lack of concern for curriculum development for schools attended by children of the working classes, confirmed, for example, by those who opposed the teaching of writing on the grounds that 'such a degree of knowledge might produce in them a disrelish for the laborious occupations of life'. During the years following the Revised Code of 1862 'the exclusive concern of most schools was to secure that children acquired a minimum standard of proficiency in reading, writing and arithmetic'. In the last forty years, and particularly since 1918, 'the outlook of the primary school has been broadened and humanized'.[9]

The 1931 Report did not represent a complete commitment to a child-centred curriculum or pedagogy, but it contained a broad endorsement of that approach. The primary school ethos, it declared,

> appeals less to passive obedience and more to the sympathy, social spirit and imagination of the children, relies less on mass instruction and more on the encouragement of individual and group work . . . It is not primarily a question

of so planning the curriculum as to convey a minimum standard of knowledge, indispensable though knowledge is, and necessary as is the disciplined application by which knowledge alone can be acquired . . . Hitherto the general tendency has been to take for granted the existence of certain traditional 'subjects' and to present them to the pupils as lessons to be mastered . . . What is required: at least so far as much of the curriculum is concerned, is to substitute for it methods which take as the starting-point of the work of the primary school the experience, the curiosity, and the awakening powers and interests of the children themselves . . . Applying these considerations to the problem before us, we see that the curriculum is to be thought of in terms of activity and experience rather than of knowledge to be acquired and facts to be stored.[10]

This concern to limit the influence of subjects, bodies of knowledge organized according to adult experience, in favour of learning based upon the more immediate experiences of children themselves, continued for more than half a century. In 1967 it was restated in *Children and their Primary Schools*, the Plowden Report. One of the major recommendations of this report was an extension of primary curricula and teaching practices by the redesignation of schools, for example, into First (5 to 8 years) and Middle (9 to 13). Then the tide turned. Two publications of 1969, *Perspectives on Plowden* edited by Richard Peters, and the first of the Black Papers, *Fight for Education*, brought the whole curriculum and ethos of primary education into question, and paved the way for a new emphasis upon subjects.

Although the main focus of curriculum debate in the twentieth century has been on the secondary school, the most distinctive feature of that curriculum has been its unchanging nature. The Education Act of 1902, which established maintained secondary schools under local education authority control, led in 1904 to regulations which prescribed the curricula for such schools. The purpose of such regulations was to provide a general curriculum to age 16 or beyond, with courses of instruction that would be complete in themselves, and not simply introductory or superficial. Minimum hours of instruction per week for each subject were prescribed, although such detailed prescription was removed in 1907. The resemblance between the secondary school curriculum of 1904 and the National Curriculum of 1988 is apparent from the following list:

1904	*1988*
English	English
Mathematics	Mathematics
Science	Science
Foreign Language	Foreign Language
Geography	Geography
History	History
Drawing	Art
Physical Exercise	Physical Education
Manual Work/Housewifery	Technology
[Music]	Music

Music, excluded from the original list of 1904, was subsequently added. Though Latin was not specified in 1904, its inclusion, together with that of a modern foreign language, was expected. Indeed, approval of the Board of Education had to be secured if two languages other than English were offered and neither was Latin. The effect of the 1904 regulations was to cast maintained secondary schools in the grammar school mould. The higher grade schools, upthrusts from the elementary system, some of which had developed a scientific and vocational dimension for the purpose of securing grants from the now defunct Science and Art Department, were abolished. Something of their curriculum and ethos, however, continued in the central schools, which provided commercial and industrial courses, and proved popular with many working-class parents and pupils.

Secondary schools were catering for two types of pupils. Some would remain to age 18, and go on to further study either in higher education or in the professions; others would leave at age 16 and proceed to the world of work. The Board of Education encouraged vocational training in school for this latter group, for example in agricultural, domestic or commercial subjects, but most secondary grammar schools, themselves staffed by graduates, continued to emphasise the traditional academic curriculum. Neither cookery mistresses nor woodwork masters, or their subjects, enjoyed high status in such schools.

The Hadow Report of 1926 provided a solution to this dilemma. It recommended two types of secondary schools – grammar, and modern. While grammar schools would continue to provide an academic, subject-based curriculum, modern secondary schools would provide four-year courses to age 15. Though such courses might take cognizance of local employment opportunities, the report emphasised that even in the final year curricula should not be 'merely vocational or utilitarian'. Instead courses would be essentially 'simpler and more limited in scope than those in Grammar Schools'. The term 'merely', confirmed the continuation of traditional hierarchies of knowledge. Nevertheless the report waxed lyrically about the curriculum of the modern school, whose pupils would flourish

> under the stimulus of practical work and realistic studies, and yet, at the same time, in the free and broad air of a general and humane education, which, if it remembers handwork, does not forget music and if it cherishes natural science fosters also linguistic and literary studies.[11]

In 1938 the Spens Report deplored the failure of the Board of Education 'to foster the development of schools of a quasi-vocational type', but rejected the concept of the multilateral school. Although a similar curriculum for the first two years of all secondary schools was proposed, grammar schools would continue with the academic curriculum, modern schools with the watered-down version, while there would be an increase in the numbers of secondary technical schools. By the 1940s there were some 200 technical schools in England; Germany had 2,000. In 1943 the Norwood Report confirmed the desirability of the tripartite divisions of English secondary education, and proposed three types of curricula: an academic curriculum for those interested in learning for its own sake, a vocational curriculum for those destined for craft and technical employment, and a general curriculum (yet to be fully developed) for the pupil who 'deals more easily with concrete things than ideas'. These three groups were to be further determined by the actual provision, in a particular area, of the three types of schools. Few secondary technical schools were built, so pupils in some parts of the country had no opportunity of access to this type of curriculum. Grammar school provision, for about 20 per cent of the population, varied considerably according to the survival of historic foundations and policies of local education authorities. Some 75 per cent of pupils in maintained secondary schools were consigned to the frequently-perceived 'elementary' curriculum, expectations and ethos of the secondary modern school.

The Education Act of 1944 said nothing about curriculum, apart from requiring religious education and a daily act of corporate worship. For the next thirty years government intervention in curriculum matters was lessened, though a number of reports continued to stress the need for more scientific and technical education, both at secondary and higher education levels. For example, in the aftermath of the Second World War, the Percy Report of 1945 and the Barlow Report of 1946 both advocated a substantial and rapid expansion of higher scientific and technological education in colleges and universities. In the 1950s further impetus was provided by the growing scientific and technological achievements of the USA and the USSR. A White Paper of 1956 recommended an expansion of technical education at all levels. From 1964 the Schools Council for the Curriculum and Examinations, a body with strong teacher representation, produced reports, recommendations and teaching materials on many topics, including the primary school curriculum and the curriculum for the young school leaver. One of the most interesting reports, Schools Council Enquiry I, *Young School Leavers*, published in 1968, showed that young school leavers and their parents wanted schools to provide examination success and vocational training. Head teachers of the same schools, however, when confronting the same list of twenty-four objectives, consigned examination success and 'things of direct use in jobs' to the lowest places.

The reorganization of the majority of maintained secondary schools along comprehensive lines generated considerable controversy, but little attention was paid to curricular matters. The ideal of the grammar school continued, indeed comprehensives were sometimes lauded as grammar schools for all, and much effort was devoted to building up traditional sixth forms, with pupils studying academic subjects for GCE 'A'-level.

In 1976, in a speech at Ruskin College, James Callaghan showed the politicians' willingness to grasp the curriculum nettle. Callaghan, one of the few modern prime minsters not to have attended university himself, publicly regretted that many graduates 'had no desire or intention of joining industry'. He also signalled the need for a core curriculum and urged that all school leavers should be fully equipped 'to do a job of work'. From 1979 Conservative governments entered the secret garden of the curriculum with a vengeance. In 1981 a Department of Education and Science circular required all local education authorities to produce curriculum policy statements. These were carefully collected and locked away, and central government then proceeded with two broad strategies.

The first was to provide training or work experience for all young people aged between 16 and 18 who were neither in education nor employment. In 1983 the Youth Training Scheme (YTS) replaced the Youth Opportunities Programme (YOP), and in the same year a Technical and Vocational Education Initiative (TVEI) was launched within schools, followed by a Certificate of Pre-Vocational Education (CPVE) in 1985. In 1986 a National Council for Vocational Qualifications (NCVQ) was established.

Kenneth Baker, who became Secretary of State in 1986, continued the theme of vocational education in schools with the announcement of the establishment of some twenty City Technology Colleges (CTCs). The major thrust of his policy, however, was to ensure a traditional subject-based curriculum for all pupils in maintained schools. Significantly, the first twenty-five clauses of the Education Reform Act of 1988 were devoted to the establishment of a National Curriculum, designed to provide a broadly-based curriculum for all and to raise standards across the whole maintained school population. Since that date much of the debate about curriculum has centred on issues arising from the nature and implementation of that curriculum.

CONCLUSION

Five conclusions may be drawn from the application of historical perspectives to the curriculum.

The first is the continuation of certain curriculum diversities and hierarchies across the centuries. Social, religious and vocational education was characteristic of the medieval and early modern periods, although the roots of subject-based schooling were also clearly visible. Child-centred approaches to education and to the curriculum also have a long history, and in the early nineteenth century were exemplified in the writings and practice of such pioneers of infant education as Robert Owen and Samuel Wilderspin. By the 1970s the child-centred approach was being increasingly identified with low standards and self-indulgence, on the part of teachers and pupils alike. Such blanket identification is dangerous in the extreme. At various points in English history a more child-centred curriculum, one which concentrates upon learning rather than upon teaching, has been shown to be advantageous. In 1993 *Learning to Succeed*, the report of the National Commission on Education, warned against some aspects of whole-class teaching and provided examples of the benefits (and of some of the problems) associated with independent and flexible learning approaches.

Unfortunately, while in other countries considerable accommodation between vocational, subject-based and child-centred education has been achieved, in England the contest is as keen as it has ever been. The contemporary separation of subject-based and vocational is reflected in SCAA and NCVQ, just as it was in the nineteenth century by the Education Department and the Science and Art Department. The GCE 'A'-level, the 'gold standard' to be preserved at all costs, represents the most obvious example of the continuing place of academic subjects in the curriculum hierarchy.

A second continuity, and hierarchy, is apparent in central government control of curriculum. As with Robert Lowe in 1867, Kenneth Baker advised that he did not think it would be right to impose the National Curriculum on independent schools. Teachers and parents in such schools could be trusted to produce an acceptable (i.e. traditional academic) curriculum. The term 'National Education', as employed in the nineteenth century, did not mean education for the whole nation, but rather an education organized and directed by the wealthy and powerful for the poor and unimportant. Recent revisions of the National Curriculum suggest that far from extending into the 16–19 age range and into independent schools, curriculum direction is reverting to the elementary age range once more.

Although the broad principle of a national curriculum currently enjoys widespread support, the dangers of centrally prescribed curricula are also apparent. These dangers may be exacerbated by fundamental contradictions. For example a national curriculum is clearly at odds with the Conservative doctrine of choice and diversity in education. Though a national curriculum may produce considerable benefits, as the experience of the Revised Code showed damage may also occur, particularly when curricula and teaching methods are too closely tied to assessment. The end result of such prescription may be the negation of true education. Both teacher and pupil become mechanical parts of a system of instruction beyond their control.

A third conclusion is that continuities in terms of contests, divisions and hierarchies are ripe for challenge. A substantial redefinition of the relationship between vocational and academic is long overdue: at the post-14 level and in curriculum and assessment bodies. The redesignation in the summer of 1995 of the Department for Education as the Department for Education and Employment may be the precursor of change in this direction. None of us knows what skills he or she will be required to exercise in adult life. In the seventeenth century John Locke advised that even the gentleman's son should learn a trade, lest he should fall on hard times, advice as appropriate today as it was then. A genuine acceptance of an entitlement curriculum for all might do something to eradicate the long-standing divide in England between high and low culture, and high and low curricula and attainments. Such a divide has not been so marked in other countries, including other parts of the United Kingdom.

Though there are continuities, there have also been changes. The religious dimensions of schooling, which included a central core of Christian learning as the most important preparation for life both in this world and in the next, have been substantially weakened. The general acceptance of the centrality of Christianity, so strong a feature of English history from the medieval period until the nineteenth century and beyond, is not reflected in the England of the 1990s. Christian (or other) faith still pervades the curriculum and ethos of a minority of schools in England. For the majority, however, there are considerable difficulties in implementing the requirements of religious education and collective worship contained in the Education Reform Act of 1988. Given the difficulties experienced by schools in adhering to similar requirements under the Butler Act of 1944, it would appear unlikely that such arrangements will provide a sufficient basis for that moral and spiritual education enjoined under the 1988 Act.

One means of indicating change in the relationship between the moral and knowledge elements of the curriculum is provided by a consideration of the terms 'vocation' and 'vocational'. Vocation implied a calling – to the service of God or of the human race. It was particularly applied to those who had dedicated their lives to God, for example as missionaries, nuns or priests. It also, by extension, was used to describe those, such as doctors, nurses and teachers, who sought in their working lives to promote the welfare of others and, in so doing, to make some sacrifice in terms of their own personal wealth and well-being. But during the nineteenth century the term 'vocational', which had previously been applied to the exercise of one's vocation, whether in a caring profession or otherwise, took on another connotation. Vocational education was frequently contrasted with other, supposedly superior, types of education which might be described as 'academic' or 'liberal'. Today the term 'vocational education' has acquired a meaning very different from that of preparation for selfless service to God and to the human race. Vocational education is now generally applied in respect of what are perceived to be low-status and far from philanthropic occupations, for example, bricklayers, hairdressers, motor mechanics. Indeed, today the term 'vocational training' is more prevalent than that of vocational education, reflecting the acquisition of specific manual skills rather than the acquisition of professional knowledge and judgement.

Finally, it is apparent from the historical perspective that things are not always what they seem. The National Curriculum, presented by Kenneth Baker as a radical reform, was in terms of control, extent, content and form, firmly rooted in the English past. It was essentially backward- rather than forward-looking, an attempt to preserve under the guise of change. It was the curriculum of Balfour and of Morant, Conservatives of the first decade of the twentieth century. It lacked a substantial rationale and justification in terms of contemporary English society, and in consequence its outcomes may be rather different from those intended by its authors. Though the National Curriculum, and its many problems of overload and amendment, have produced considerable difficulties, not least for pupils, parents, teachers and educational publishers, one substantial concept has emerged – that of entitlement. If the National Curriculum is to be broadly construed, such entitlement has implications not only for quantity and quality of subject content, but also for the quantity and quality of teachers, buildings, equipment and other resources. To the curriculum historian the importance of reform frequently lies not so much in its achievements as in its symbolism, particularly as reflected back into culture and society. The National Curriculum has raised expectations about national education which may render the government's proposed five-year moratorium on curriculum change completely ineffective.

NOTES

1. Lawton, 1975, 6–7.
2. Quoted in Aldrich, 1991, 95.
3. SCAA, 1994, 7.
4. Parker, 1914, 160.

5. Quoted in Reeder, 1980, 123.
6. Quoted in Maclure, 1969, 110.
7. Quoted in Maclure, 1969, 108.
8. Quoted in Maclure, 1969, 111.
9. Quoted in Maclure, 1969, 189.
10. Quoted in Maclure, 1969, 189–92.
11. Quoted in Maclure, 1969, 181.

SUGGESTED READING

Goodson, I. (ed.) (1985) *Social Histories of the Secondary Curriculum.*
Goodson, I. and Ball, S. (eds) (1984) *Defining the Curriculum: Histories and Ethnographies.*
Gordon, P. and Lawton, D. (1978) *Curriculum Change in the Nineteenth and Twentieth Centuries.*
Graham, D. (with Tytler, D.) (1993) *A Lesson for Us All: the Making of the National Curriculum.*
Haft, H. and Hopmann, S. (eds) (1990) *Case Studies in Curriculum Administration History.*
Lawton, D. (1975) *Class, Culture and the Curriculum.*
Lawton, D. and Chitty, C. (eds) (1988) *The National Curriculum.*

THREE

Standards and Assessment

CURRENT ISSUES

International comparisons indicate that the levels of attainment reached by school-children in England fall considerably short of those achieved by their counterparts in other countries. Research by Green and Steedman, quoted in the report of the National Commission on Education, showed that between 1990 and 1991 the proportions of 16-year-olds achieving the equivalent of GCSE grades A–C in mathematics, the national language and a science, in France, Germany and Japan were 66, 62 and 50 per cent respectively. In England the figure was only 27 per cent. Over the same period, the percentages of young people aged 18 years and above obtaining an upper secondary school qualification in France, Germany and Japan were 48, 68 and 80 respectively. In England the figure was a mere 29 per cent.[1]

Since 1945 basic standards of literacy and numeracy have shown little change. Among 7- and 8-year-olds reading standards fell slightly in the 1980s, although there was no change in writing standards. Reading standards of 11- and 15-year-olds showed slight rises around 1950 and in the 1980s, but overall have changed little. Such pupils also showed a fall in number skills between 1982 and 1987, but a rise in geometry, measures and statistics.[2]

Monitoring of standards over time is difficult. If the same test is used it may not reflect changes in school syllabuses and priorities; where different tests are used issues of direct comparability arise. Although the introduction of National Curriculum assessment at ages 7, 11 and 14, and the development of public examinations at 16 and 18 will provide substantial evidence about the performance of pupils and of schools, such evidence is not necessarily the best means of monitoring changes in standards of attainment. The National Commission's proposal to establish an Educational Achievement Unit, based on the former Assessment of Performance Unit but covering the whole of the United Kingdom, was an attempt to meet this need.

In recent years government strategies to address the shortcomings of English education and to raise standards of attainment have centred upon centrally directed assessment. The Education Reform Act of 1988 made provision for a national assessment programme to accompany that of a national curriculum. Under the programme pupils were to be assessed against predetermined 'attainment targets'; by their teachers continuously and by external tests called Standard Assessment Tasks (SATs) at the ages of 7, 11, 14 and 16. The results of these tests at school level were to be publicly reported (at 11, 14 and 16).

Although implementation of the new arrangements was subject to considerable disruption and modification, the principle of setting attainment targets at national level as a means of improving the standards of English education gained wide acceptance. In February 1994 the government announced that by 1997 80 per cent of young people would be expected to achieve five GCSE passes at grades A to C or the equivalent National Vocational Qualification level 2. A target of 60 per cent of young people with NVQ level 3 (two 'A'-levels or the equivalent) has been set for the year 2000.[3]

Assessment pervades modern society. We live in the age of the calculable human being. People are assessed at every stage in their lives: for example as children for and in education, as adults for and in employment. Knowledge and skills must be assessed and certificated. This is not only mandatory for those, like doctors, engineers or airline pilots, upon whose professional skills the lives of other human beings depend. Any person wishing to take a car or motor cycle onto the public highway must also submit to a formal assessment of his or her competence to drive.

Within the education system assessment takes several forms. Some occurs inside the classroom, and is under the direct control of the teacher – question and answer sessions, written work completed in school or for homework. External examinations, for example General Certificate of Secondary Education (GCSE) at age 16, and General Certificate of Education at Advanced level (GCE 'A') at age 18, provide assessment which is controlled from outside the school. Such assessment, however, has not, as in other countries, been controlled directly by the central authority, but has been in the hands of university boards and other autonomous and semi-autonomous bodies.

Assessment serves several functions in the educational process: screening (to identify pupils with special educational needs); diagnosis (to determine the strengths and weaknesses of individual pupils); record keeping (to keep track of levels and changes over time); feedback (to furnish information about the performance of pupils, classes, teachers, schools and local education authorities); certification (to supply a guarantee that a pupil has reached a certain level of competence or knowledge); and selection (to determine entry into further stages of education or employment).[4] These functions may be classified into two broad groups: professional or 'formative' – helping the teacher in the educational process; managerial or 'summative' – assisting the management of the education system (on the basis of results).[5]

Current issues include those of national assessment, league tables, GCSE and GCE 'A'-level.

National assessment has had a chequered career. The principle of regular testing, based upon nationally approved criteria, which provoked considerable resistance when introduced in 1988, now commands widespread support. In 1993 the then Secretary of State for Education, John Patten, argued that:

> it is in the interests of properly taught children, informed parents, employers and the nation as a whole for the testing arrangements . . . to go ahead without interruption. If not we will have an education system without adequate rigour, and will have conceded a decade's advantage to our international competitors.[6]

Nevertheless, although by 1993 the principle of national assessment was broadly accepted, the details of the actual scheme continued to cause concern. Justification for such concern was provided by a report from the Office for Standards in Education (OFSTED) which declared the English tests of that year for 14-year-olds to be of 'dubious quality', criticized the overall system of national assessment as 'too complicated' with 'weaknesses in practice', and confirmed that 'only one in 20 schools took the tests for 14-year-olds in English, mathematics and science'. Some of the English papers were deemed by the inspectors to have 'constituted an invalid assessment of pupils' attainment'.[7]

Teacher criticism of the tests, which led to widespread boycotts, focused not only upon the invalid nature of parts of the process, but also upon the inordinate amount of time spent by pupils and teachers upon assessment, as opposed to learning and teaching.

National assessment was designed to provide hard evidence about the quality of work in English schools and to identify successful and failing pupils, teachers and schools. This information was to be made public, so that good schools would drive out bad. League tables of school results, at GCSE and 'A'-level, are now an accepted part of the educational scene, and are published in national as well as local newspapers. In 1994, David Blunkett, the Labour Party's shadow Education Secretary, declared his support for the publication of test and examination results.[8] The issue, however, has shifted from whether such results should be published, to the form in which they should appear. Advocates of 'valued-added' tables stress the importance of comparing the performance of individual pupils and schools over time, and of measuring attainment at entry to, and exit levels from, a school.

Controversies surrounding the GCSE examination are of two kinds. The first suggests that the general standard of GCSE is too low for those pupils who were previously stretched by GCE Ordinary level, hence the introduction of a starred A grade in 1994. Rhodes Boyson has argued that 'It is impossible to mark over a total ability range.'[9] The second focuses upon the nature of the assessment. In 1991 John Major himself attacked GCSE in a speech to the Centre for Policy Studies, declaring that 'It is clear that there is now too much coursework, project work and teacher assessment in GCSE. The remedy surely lies in getting GCSE back to being an externally assessed exam, which is predominantly written.'[10]

As for Advanced level, the main controversy centres upon the very existence of this examination, which has long been used as a means of selection for entry to higher education. On the one hand are those who believe that 'A'-level is sacrosanct, a 'gold standard' to which other courses, including the new National Vocational

Qualifications, should aspire. The National Commission on Education, however, was but one voice in the chorus that proclaimed that 'A'-levels are too restrictive, and recommended a General Education Diploma at Advanced level in its stead. Such a diploma, together with an Ordinary level, normally taken at age 16, would replace the current multiplicity of assessment mechanisms, and include both vocational and academic qualifications. The Report of the National Commission advocated a diploma with many subjects and many pathways as a means of bringing

> to an end the increasingly sterile debate about 'parity of esteem' between the different qualifications available at ages 16–18. It should also give a new dimension to the narrow academic experience which 'A' levels force on so many academically able young people.[11]

Another criticism of 'A'-level is that unlike GCSE and NVQs which are criterion-referenced – with an objective set of standards against which pupils' performances are measured – 'A'-levels are still largely norm-referenced. Under such a system a norm of, for example, 50 per cent of the marks is identified and a candidate's performance is measured against the norm and against those of other candidates.

Finally, in this section, it must be noted that assessment in higher education is also causing considerable concern. The rapid transition from an elite to a mass system has raised fears that standards have been reduced. In the late nineteenth and early years of the twentieth century, some university departments refused, on principle, in the first ten years to give a first-class degree, so that a reputation for rigour might be established. In spite of the massive increase in numbers of universities and of university students in the 1990s, such self-denying ordinances no longer obtain, and first-class degrees proliferate.

HISTORICAL PERSPECTIVES

Although it is natural to think of formal assessment as a phenomenon which has developed in modern times, it is salutary to observe that a most elaborate system of examinations to determine entry into the Chinese imperial service existed for some 1,500 years until the second half of the nineteenth century. Success in these examinations involved survival through a series of competitions spread over several years.

The first set of examinations, which comprised some ten heats, led eventually to the bachelor's degree, with a further series for that of master. Neither of these two qualifications, however, gave entry to public employment in the higher offices of state. The final series was held in Peking, after which successful candidates were allocated to posts by lot. Yet further heats took place for those who wished to obtain the highest posts, as Court poets or historians, or as provincial examiners. The examinations were competitive, rather than norm-referenced, and the syllabuses changed in accordance with changes in society. Early concentration upon military and physical accomplishments gave way to a greater emphasis upon literate and administrative skills. While most Chinese males (though not the sons of such occupations as actors or torturers) were eligible to enter the contest, and thus provided a means of some social mobility, the numbers of successful candidates were so few that no radical changes to the social structure ensued.

For most of English history status and position were determined by birth and sex, as opposed to achievement and qualifications. Nevertheless, in medieval times entry to certain occupations did require the successful completion of prescribed tests. The Universities of Oxford and Cambridge and some craft and trade guilds required those who wished to attain the rank of master to submit themselves to examination.

> Tests of competence were required of students or apprentices; further tests or 'masterpieces' were required of bachelors or journeymen before they were admitted to the full brotherhood. One suspects that something more than mere technical competence may have been necessary: acceptability or even orthodoxy may have been the price of becoming an insider. University men proceeded by degrees and emphasis was laid as much upon attendance at courses as upon successful testing.[12]

By the later eighteenth century, however, the term 'apprentice' was being used in a much wider range of occupations, including those for which no final test or assessment was required. At the same time the assessment procedures of the two English universities had become little more than empty formalities.

Nineteenth century

University reform began at Cambridge where the mathematical tripos were introduced between 1747 and 1750. In 1752 an honours list was published, with candidates divided into three classes: wranglers, senior optimes, junior optimes. By the end of the century written papers were being used in examining for fellowships at some Cambridge colleges. These included questions on such subjects as geography and history, but overall, mathematics continued to take pride of place, so that it was not until 1822 that the second tripos examination, in classics, was established. Entry was restricted to those who had already completed the mathematics tripos. At Oxford reform stemmed from the Public Examination Statute of 1800, which gave classics primacy of place over mathematics. In 1807 a further reform divided all candidates who achieved the honours standard into classes; previously there had been a single unclassified list of only twelve honours graduates. Subsequent development saw the addition of new subjects for examination, for example in moral sciences and natural sciences at Cambridge from 1848, and in law and modern history, and natural sciences at Oxford from 1850. Some areas remained untouched by reform, however. Both at Oxford and at Cambridge the master's degree continued to be available without examination.

There were some who inveighed against the unfortunate effects of the new examinations: the tendency to cram at the expense of true education, the sacrifice of original study and of original thought, the overpressure which afflicted conscientious students, the inaccuracies and unfairness of the system, the extraordinary (and at times unwarranted) prestige that might be attached to those who were placed at the top of the honours lists. On balance, however, there can be little doubt that the introduction of a formal written examination system was of considerable benefit to the intellectual well-being of both universities. Since most of the teaching was still at college, rather than university level, competition ensued not only between the individual candidates, but also between the colleges.

The most important development in respect of examinations in higher education occurred with the foundation of the University of London. This title was originally assumed in 1828 by the institution which became University College, London when in 1836 the current University of London was established as the body to provide examinations and degrees for its two constituent colleges – University and King's. From 1858 the University of London opened its external examinations, and degrees, to students not only in England, but around the world. This extension made it possible for a variety of nascent institutions of higher education which did not yet have the power to grant degrees to prepare their students for the examinations of a university with a worldwide reputation. Such separation of examination from teaching earned the scorn of many, like J. H. Newman, who himself failed to secure the expected first-class degree, and whose idea of a university was founded upon a residential college and the pursuit of knowledge for its own sake.

During the nineteenth century most secondary schools, both for boys and girls, were private establishments. Proprietors and head teachers in good schools urgently sought a means of proving their worth to the public. One method of so doing was to pay for an inspection by a cleric or university don, but given the spread of examinations in other spheres of society – in universities, the professions, government departments, even in the elementary school – some more public means of displaying worth, and of providing a focus and purpose of study was sought.

Although the universities also played a leading role in the provision of examinations for secondary schools, the original impulse for such examinations came from the College of Preceptors, founded in 1846 and granted a royal charter some three years later. One of the original purposes of the College was to provide examinations and qualifications for teachers, so that the public might have a guarantee of their learning and competence. Sadly, but predictably, most teachers were happier to submit pupils rather than themselves to such ordeals. In 1850 the College conducted an examination of boys at the Standard Hill Academy in Nottingham. Candidates were classified in three divisions, and from 1853 a general system was in operation with written papers and a board of examiners. Girls were admitted to the examinations, although at first they sat separate papers from the boys. In 1872 girls won two of the major prizes, including that for classics, while by 1879 the College was annually examining more than 8,000 candidates (with a subject entry of some 40–50,000).[13] From 1856 the Royal Society of Arts, founded in 1754 for the purpose of promoting art, commerce, industry and invention, also began a series of examinations for older school pupils, while two years later the Universities of Oxford and Cambridge entered the field with their 'local' examinations. League tables of school examination successes soon began to appear in the educational press.

Secondary school examinations of the second half of the nineteenth century enabled pupils from private schools to compete against those from endowed grammar and other ancient foundations. They also allowed girls to compete against boys, and in so doing prompted significant change in the curricula of many girls' schools. Moreover, once girls had demonstrated success in secondary school examinations it was more difficult to resist their entry into higher education. By the end of the century, however, it was increasingly observed that there was too much competition between the several examining bodies; both the Taunton and Bryce Commissions commented on the need to provide greater coherence. Schools, however, were wary of central government interference in this field, and preferred to remain under the aegis of such bodies as the universities and College of Preceptors.

During the nineteenth century competitive entry based upon examinations came to replace patronage as the means of recruitment to many posts in the professions and public services. Professions, old and new, from solicitors to accountants, introduced examinations to regulate entry into their ranks. From 1854 entry to the Indian Civil Service was made subject to competitive examination, while the Northcote–Trevelyan Report of the same year recommended the establishment of a central board of examiners to oversee recruitment into all branches of the civil service. The Civil Service Commission was set up in 1855, but the general opening of public service, both civil and military, to competitive entry had to await the reforms of the Gladstone government of 1868–74. Competitive entry to the professions and public service led to two developments. The first was the growth of crammers specifically devoted to preparation for a particular test, for example the entry examination to Woolwich for those proceeding to a military career. The second was the creation of separate 'modern' sides or forms within schools in which curricula and teaching were tailored to entrance examinations and employment of a general or specific nature.

Central government intervention in assessment came through inspection and examination. From 1839 government inspectors were appointed to oversee grants of money to the school societies. Their role was to visit schools to ensure that such money was being spent effectively. From 1846 their duties included conducting the annual examinations of pupil teachers, and of teachers seeking to secure a government certificate. From 1862 the role of inspectors underwent substantial change with the introduction of the Revised Code. Though the original proposal to base all grants to schools on the performance of pupils in annual examinations was modified (up to four shillings per child was to be paid for attendance, as opposed to eight shillings on examination) the basic principle of payment by results was adopted. Henceforth the salaries of teachers, together with the general income of the school, would depend upon the examination of children in reading, writing and arithmetic under six standards. Detailed instructions were issued to inspectors as to the conduct of the examinations. Reading, which was examined individually, and the slate work of younger children in writing and arithmetic, had to be marked in the school. The writing and arithmetic of older pupils which was done on paper might be marked by the inspector in school or taken away, but all work completed on paper had to be sent, with a copy of the complete mark schedule, to the Education Department. Six grades were established: excellent, good, fair, moderate, imperfect and failure, with a pass mark being awarded to the highest three grades. The six standards established in 1862, which might roughly be taken to correspond to children aged between 6 and 11, were as shown in Table 3.1.

Table 3.1

	Standard I	*Standard II*	*Standard III*	*Standard IV*	*Standard V*	*Standard VI*
Reading	Narrative in monosyllables	One of the narratives next in order after monosyllables in an elementary reading book used in the school.	A short paragraph from an elementary reading book used in the school	A short paragraph from a more advanced reading book used in the school.	A few lines of poetry from a reading book used in the first class in the school.	A short ordinary paragraph in a newspaper, or other modern narrative.
Writing	Form on blackboard or slate from dictation, letters capital and small manuscript.	Copy in manuscript character a line of print.	A sentence from the same paragraph, slowly read once, and then dictated in single words.	A sentence slowly dictated once by a few words at a time from the same book, but not from the paragraph read.	A sentence slowly dictated once, by a few words at a time, from a reading book used in the first class of the school.	Another short ordinary paragraph in a newspaper, or other modern narrative, slowly dictated once by a few words at a time.
Arithmetic	Form on blackboard or slate, from dictation, figures up to 20: name at sight figures up to 20: add and subtract figures up to 10, orally, and from examples on blackboard.	A sum in simple addition and subtraction, and the multiplication table.	A sum in any simple rule as far as short division (inclusive).	A sum in compound rules (money).	A sum in compound rules (common weights and measures).	A sum in practice or bills of parcels.

Examples of the arithmetic questions presented to children in a Wiltshire school in 1864 were:

Standard I
Add 4+2+3; subtract 7–5; write down 17.

Standard II
Add 406+18+390+7; subtract 342–89; write out the 8 times multiplication table.

Standard III
Add 2416+305+7049+4003; subtract 3418–349; divide 4672 by 9.

Standard IV
Add £24,108 5s 11½d + £1,919 12s 11½d; multiply £78,416 2s 5½d by 8; divide £31,763 14s 9¾d by 8.

In each case two of the three answers had to be correct to secure a pass. Pass rates were as follows:[14]

Table 3.2

			Passed in:	
Standard	Children presented	Arithmetic	Reading	Writing
I	37	35	21	35
II	17	3	10	17
III	17	12	17	16
IV	5	4	5	3
Total:	76	54	53	71

Defenders of the Revised Code maintained that it was now in the interest of the teachers that all children in a class should learn, and that the attainments of young children were as important as those of older pupils. They also defended the concentration upon basic subjects, arguing that until these were placed at the heart of school instruction once more, other subjects such as geography and history were rightly relegated to subordinate positions. In spite of the rigours of the Code pupil numbers in government-assisted elementary schools continued to grow, and from 1867 grants were given for examinations in a wider range of subjects.

Opponents of payment by results deplored the narrowing of the curriculum and of the methods of instruction, regretted the effects upon the role and status of teachers and training colleges, and criticized the perfunctory nature of the examination. For example, in 1864 HMI Revd W. Hernaman spent one and a quarter hours at Clifton-on-Teme School during which time he examined sixty-two children in five standards in arithmetic, reading and writing and also inspected them in religious knowledge and the Catechism.[15] When examinations were conducted with such speed even the merest hesitation over a few words by a child could result in failure in reading.

From its inception in 1862 there had been severe criticisms of the system of payment by results, but some thirty years elapsed before there was general agreement that the disadvantages outweighed the advantages. Substantial modifications occurred from 1890, while annual examinations were abolished from 1895. By 1900 a block grant was in operation, and elementary schools were once again subject to general, rather than examination-based, inspection.

The Report of the Committee of Council on Education, 1897–98, in justifying the abandonment of the annual examination and payment by results, provided an analysis of the weaknesses of taking one method of assessment as an overall judgement, whether of schools or pupils, which is as applicable in the twentieth century, and beyond, as it was in the nineteenth.

> It was our aim to relieve efficient schools and teachers from the false standard of educational excellence which the old system of examination tended to set up. We believe that a teacher who is competent for his duties and zealous in their discharge does his work best when he is given freedom in the choice of methods and liberty to adapt his course of instruction to the needs and abilities of his pupils. The most permanent and valuable results of education are not those which can be elaborately displayed on an annual field day. It is misleading to attempt to measure a teacher's educational skill or the more lasting effects of his instruction on the faculties and character of his pupils by a test which tends to throw the chief stress on the reproduction of a certain amount of knowledge on an appointed day. Such a system inevitably encourages sham rather than true education. It sets a premium on kinds of special preparation which are generally incompatible with the necessarily slow and less showy processes of thorough intellectual discipline. Children can usually be made to acquire, for a temporary purpose, a great deal of information which is afterwards quickly forgotten, and leaves behind it little permanent impress or lasting good. We are far from wishing to underrate the discipline involved, alike for teachers and pupils, in having to accomplish a given task by a given date. The duty of preparing for an appointed examination is within certain limits salutary in its influence on the work of all concerned. A definite aim stimulates them to orderly and systematic effort, and forms the habit of punctual preparation for an appointed test. But a system which makes this the chief aim of school-work is hurtful to the true efficiency of educational effort. It assesses its merits by a false standard. It induces superficial and fleeting excellence. It fixes attention on some of the less important results of the educational process, and too little on the educational process itself . . . A school is a living thing, and should be judged as a living thing, not merely as a factory producing a certain modicum of examinable knowledge.[16]

Another series of central government grants to schools, based on examinations, were those administered by the Science and Art Department between 1853 and 1899. Grants were given both to teachers and to pupils who passed examinations in a range of subjects, from drawing to zoology. By 1873 examinations were being provided in twenty-three subjects. Though grants were not intended for pupils in elementary schools, higher elementary and higher grade schools established by school boards under the Education Act of 1870 were particular beneficiaries of Science and Art Department grants, as were the technical colleges, science schools and evening institutes which mushroomed in the last years of the nineteenth century. In 1892 there were 214,000 entries in science and 123,700 entries in art.[17]

Twentieth century

One of the most notable features of the English educational scene in the new century was the maintained secondary school. Methods of assessing standards of entry to, and exit from, such schools became a matter of public and professional concern. The Free Place Regulations of 1907, which gave increased grants to local education authority maintained secondary schools, stipulated that a minimum of 25 per cent of places in these schools should be reserved for pupils from public elementary schools. Selection of such pupils would be by a scholarship or free-place examination. Between the wars 11 was adopted as the normal age at which pupils transferred from elementary to grammar schools, while the 11-plus examination became the means of assessing which pupils should be selected.

In the nineteenth century intelligence testing had been developed in a number of countries, particularly as a means of classifying children (and adults) into various categories of mental deficiency. From 1917 it was employed to assess the abilities and suitabilities of American army recruits. The application of intelligence testing to selection for entry to grammar schools rested upon a growing belief in the need (and the ability) to assess basic levels of intelligence rather than of achievement. A belief in the relative permanence of an individual's Intelligence Quotient (IQ) not only provided greater assurance that children who performed well in such tests at age 11 would continue to do so throughout their school careers, it also encouraged the view that an IQ level (120 or above) appropriate to a grammar school education could be determined. Accordingly, during the inter-war years local education authorities increasingly incorporated intelligence tests into their selection procedures, while streaming according to ability became a feature of many primary schools. No uniformity, however, emerged. As Sutherland has shown

> it was possible for English educational authorities to be somewhat selective and cavalier in their reception of mental measurement. Some treated it as a useful propaganda device. Others treated it like a new toy. Yet others came to see how it might help them sophisticate and refine existing methods of selection.[18]

After the Second World War, the efficacy of assessment at age 11 became a crucial factor in the debate about comprehensive secondary schools. A wide variety of methods was still being used and even those who defended the tripartite system acknowledged that some 10 per cent of pupils were wrongly selected. Other studies also showed that coaching could substantially improve test scores.

Whereas assessment for entry to secondary schools remained under the control of local education authorities, assessment for entry to higher education, hitherto the traditional preserve of the universities themselves, now came increasingly under central government direction. In 1911 the Consultative Committee of the Board of Education proposed some reduction in the numbers of secondary school examinations and examining bodies, and in 1917 a Secondary School Examinations Council was established to act as a co-ordinating and advisory body. Its members represented university examining boards, teachers, and the local education authorities. A School Certificate Examination was established for secondary school pupils aged 16 who had undertaken a general five-year course. Candidates were required to offer at least five subjects, with a minimum of one from each of three groups – English subjects, mathematics and science, foreign languages. Five passes, including one from each group, were required for the award of a School Certificate. A fourth group, consisting originally of art and music, was added in 1923–24. A Second Examination (the Higher School Certificate) to be taken at age 18 after two years of sixth form study, allowed for specialization in one of three subject groups: classics and ancient history; modern studies; mathematics and science. The Higher Certificate served a dual purpose of providing a general assessment of pupil performance over seven years of secondary schooling and a qualification for entry to higher education and the professions.

After the Second World War, the determination of central government to play a greater role in secondary school examining was indicated by a reconstitution of the Secondary School Examinations Council, which saw the exclusion of the examining bodies. In the 1950s the School Certificate and Higher School Certificate examinations were replaced by General Certificate of Education examinations at Ordinary and Advanced levels. These forms of assessment were intended to diminish the emphasis upon assessing the whole school course, which should be a matter for schools and teachers themselves, and rather to provide a record of the attainments of individual pupils in their chosen subjects, although only three grades – distinction, pass or fail – were awarded. Scholarship papers were to be introduced to complement those at Advanced level, especially for pupils seeking State Scholarships to support them through higher education. By the 1960s grades were being awarded at both 'O'- and 'A'-levels, and what had been intended as a qualifying examination was being transformed into a competitive one. At the same time the element of competition in securing funding for undergraduate studies was reduced. From 1962 local education authorities were required to provide grants for those who secured a university place.

One of the most significant features of the assessment procedures of English education in the twentieth century was the situation which existed in elementary and secondary modern schools, whereby the majority of pupils did not obtain any form of general school-leaving certificate. While GCE examinations were intended for pupils in grammar schools, secondary age children in other schools continued to be assessed by the examinations of such long-standing bodies as the Royal Society of Arts and the College of Preceptors. A new Certificate examination for 15-year-olds was introduced by the Preceptors in 1953, while in 1957 and 1958 the RSA added a School Technical Examination and a School Certificate to the School Commercial Certificate begun as long ago as 1927. Some GCE Ordinary level work, however, did take place in secondary modern schools. In 1964 the establishment of the Schools Council for the Curriculum and Examinations marked the increasing involvement of teachers in formal assessment procedures, and from the following year a new examination, the Certificate of Secondary Education (CSE), was introduced to cater for the next 40 per cent of the ability range, GCE being considered suitable for the top 20 per cent. CSE was organized at a regional level, and afforded teachers considerable opportunities for participation and control. Three modes of assessment were offered. Mode 1 was similar to the traditional externally set examination paper; Mode 2 was an external examination set upon a syllabus provided by a school or group of schools; Mode 3 was an examination set and marked by a school or group of schools, with external moderation by the regional board.

Since 1979, and particularly since 1988, central government's re-entry into the 'secret garden' of the curriculum has been accompanied by a re-entry into that of assessment. The Schools Council was abolished in 1984, and replaced initially by separate bodies for curriculum and assessment, united in 1993 as the School Curriculum and Assessment Authority. A common examination at age 16, the General Certificate of Secondary Education, replaced the former GCE 'O'-level and CSE.

The educational reforms of the 1980s also impinged upon the assessment of technical and vocational qualifications. For most of the twentieth century, assessment in these areas had been undertaken by such bodies as the Royal Society of Arts and the City and Guilds of London Institute. The City and Guilds founded in 1878 and incorporated two years later, soon took over the technological examinations of the Royal Society of Arts, and in 1908 had more than 13,000 candidates. By 1949 these had mushroomed to 63,716 candidates in 170 subjects, and by 1975 there were 433,000 City and Guilds students following courses in more than 300 subjects. At higher levels, in addition to university degrees and courses validated by the Council for National Academic Awards (more than 1,000 in 1979–80), there were a range of Ordinary and Higher National Certificates and Diplomas. Two issues emerged. The first was to provide some standardization across the range; the second to establish some equivalence and interrelationship with academic qualifications.

Recent intervention by central government in the assessment of technical and vocational qualifications has been via the National Council for Vocational Qualifications. While GCSE boards offer a range of vocationally orientated syllabuses, National Vocational Qualifications (NVQs) assess competence to perform a particular job. In the 1990s a framework of five levels of qualification has been established, ranging from the most basic, NVQ1, through craft level (NVQ2); technician level (NVQ3); sub-degree and degree levels (NVQ4), with a potential postgraduate stage (NVQ5). The addition of general vocational qualifications (GNVQs), which relate to a number of occupational categories, is complementing NVQs and making comparison with other forms of assessment more feasible. The purpose of a GNVQ3, designed as a middle way between academic and NVQ provision, is to enable students post-16 to explore a broad vocational area, such as health and social care or business, in some depth.

CONCLUSION

Four major, but interrelated, conclusions may be drawn from the historical perspective.

The first concerns the nature of assessment. While assessment is still regularly conducted by a variety of oral methods, including interviews and practical tests, since the later eighteenth century assessment became increasingly identified with written examinations. Such written examinations now appear in a variety of forms – coursework, multiple choice tests, pre-disclosed or undisclosed papers, dissertations and theses. The development of written examinations reflected the general growth of a literate culture, but it also reflected the advantages of such examinations: the greater time given to candidates to display their attainments; the application of a standard test to all; the judgement by examiners who might have no knowledge of the candidates. These advantages were apparent in the assessments undertaken under the Revised Code. Reading had to be examined by the Inspector on the spot, individually and in a brisk manner. There was no opportunity to check or challenge his assessment. In contrast papers in arithmetic and writing could be taken by all children simultaneously, the Inspector was not required to mark such papers in the school, and his assessment could subsequently be verified by clerks in the Education Department.

Written examinations have served, and continue to serve, many purposes. At the most fundamental level they can be seen to have contributed to a substantial change in English history. Examinations were an important factor in combating the static nature and patronage of English society in the late eighteenth century, and in promoting a more competent and competitive culture. They have contributed to the rise of the meritocratic society and of the meritocratic state.

They have also contributed to the raising of standards. There can be little doubt that, overall, the public examination systems introduced into the two ancient universities in the late eighteenth and nineteenth centuries improved the levels of scholarship of both teachers and students. Recent attempts to secure a similar improvement in standards in English schools, by providing a series of regular national assessments during the school course, and by a common examination at age 16, and publication of such results, fit squarely into this tradition. The raising of standards has been advocated not only, or not principally, as a good in itself, but rather as a means of promoting a more competent and competitive culture once more.

The second conclusion relates to another function of examinations, and one closely connected with the rise of meritocracy, their use as a means of selection. National efficiency depends upon having the most competent people in positions of power and authority, and examinations may be seen, therefore, as a means of promoting both the potential social mobility of the few and the greater good of the whole. But competitive examinations have also been used as a means of exclusion. For example, examinations might be tailored to fit the products of certain educational institutions and to exclude others, by means of the inclusion of compulsory subjects such as Latin or by age requirements. Another problem which has emanated from the use of examinations for the purpose of selection, is that such examinations have required the failure of the many to secure the success of the few. Those who failed the 11-plus examination in the twentieth century and proceeded to secondary modern schools, found themselves assessed as future hewers of wood and drawers of water, almost as irredeemably as those children from the working classes whose only education was received in a nineteenth-century elementary school. Moreover, in spite of all the effort expended to ensure that intelligence rather than attainment was being assessed at transfer to secondary schools, the connection between success in written assessment and the more literate culture of professional as opposed to working-class manual families remained strong.

The use of examinations as a means of exclusion brings into focus a third major issue – that of control. In the last forty years of the nineteenth century, control over elementary school examinations was exercised by central government through its officers, Her Majesty's Inspectors, in an annual ritual which struck terror into the hearts of children, teachers and managers alike. There was something highly incongruous about these graduates of Oxford and Cambridge stalking the land to assess the performance of each and every child in an assisted school in rudimentary reading, writing and arithmetic, but the assessment process, when geared to grant allocation, provided a control mechanism without parallel. At the same time assessment in secondary schools came substantially under the control of examining bodies based upon the universities. In the twentieth century the assessment of elementary, and subsequently of secondary modern, pupils was largely conceded to schools and to teachers. In primary schools, however, a final examination, the 11-plus, was controlled by local education authorities, although frequently with teacher and school participation. While university-based examination boards continued to supply assessment for secondary school pupils at ages 16 and 18, such assessment was made subject to central government control. Though for a period of some twenty years from 1964, with the establishment of the Schools Council and the decline of the 11-plus examination, it appeared that teacher control of assessment would substantially increase, in the 1980s central government control was firmly reasserted across the years of compulsory schooling.

Those who control assessment procedures have power not only over the nature of such procedures, and therefore over the curricula, study and teaching methods of those preparing for them, whether as candidates or teachers, but also over the purposes to which they are put. Though the Revised Code of 1862 was promoted as a means of ensuring efficient learning in the basic subjects amongst elementary school pupils, it was also an administrative device by which central government could distribute grants to schools in a cheaper and more efficient manner than before. The administrative need determined the nature of the assessment, and hence of the curriculum. The example of the operation of the Revised Code and of payment by results is a salutary one. An assessment system whose principal purpose is not broadly educational, but rather administrative, financial or ideological, has considerable capacity to retard, rather than to advance educational goals, including those of raising standards. A system that is too complex may divert attention away from learning and teaching to assessment; a system that is too narrow may limit horizons and encourage teaching to the test. The greater the consequences that depend upon such assessment – for example in determining resources, either directly or as a result of pupil recruitment – the greater the likelihood of such outcomes.

Whilst the separation of those who control assessment from those who teach and learn may be justified on grounds of impartiality and objectivity, two major areas of criticism arise. The first relates to the needs of those who are to be assessed. For example, written examinations provided a unique means whereby the abilities of males and females could be submitted to a common test, so that in 1890 at a time when Cambridge University did not grant degrees to women but allowed them to sit the same examinations as men, the achievement of Philippa Fawcett, who was placed 'above Senior Wrangler', was widely acclaimed as advancing the women's cause. But submission to the same examinations as men, and to the hierarchy of knowledge which they enshrined, meant that girls' education was subject in its assessment, and consequently to a considerable extent in its curriculum, to examination authorities which were composed of males and reflected their priorities and concerns.

A second problem occurs when examinations not only come to determine the nature of education, but also may be seen as essentially antithetical to education itself. This was the conclusion reached by the Committee of Council on Education at the end of the nineteenth century, albeit it had spent some thirty-five years in establishing and administering the annual examination system which it now condemned. But the potential weaknesses of a system of assessment inherent in the separation of examining from teaching were not only evident in respect of central government and elementary schools. In outlining his ideal of a university and of a university education, Newman placed residence and tutorial superintendence above written examinations or other means of formal assessment. For Newman, an institution such as the University of London, which provided degrees to those who could pass its examinations, but took no account of the nature and circumstances in which the candidates acquired their learning, was no university at all.

Finally, what of standards? This chapter began with yet another indication that the educational standards attained by the majority of English children are poor in comparison with those in other countries. The controversies which surround standards are legion, and the historical perspective shows clearly that changes in the nature and amount of knowledge, particularly in the second half of the twentieth century, make comparisons over time both difficult and potentially misleading. Nevertheless, it is quite clear that over centuries there has been a marked improvement in certain educational standards. For example, standards of basic literacy have improved steadily since the sixteenth century, although with periods of retrogression at certain times and in certain areas, most notably in the industrializing towns of the late eighteenth and early nineteenth centuries. Similarly, since the second half of the nineteenth century the numbers of those succeeding in publicly recognized assessment procedures have steadily grown. Secondary schools and higher education continue to produce increasing numbers of graduates. While comparability of standards in such examinations over time remains a contentious issue, even if such standards are on occasion reduced, any such reduction would appear to be more than compensated for by the increased numbers of successful candidates. This is a most important development, because contemporary international comparisons confirm the historical evidence that while standards of the able minority in England are on a par with similar groups in other countries, such standards are too thinly spread.

Basic standards of literacy and numeracy, however, do not appear to have risen substantially since 1945. Although fewer than one per cent of school leavers and adults may be classified as illiterate, in the sense of being unable to read simple texts, low levels of reading and writing literacy persist in large sections of the population. Certain basic skills have probably declined. For example, knowledge of the Bible, the essential reading book of so many nineteenth-century schools, has doubtless diminished both among children and adults. Nineteenth-century copy books also show that many elementary schoolchildren learned to write a copperplate hand, and to work large arithmetical calculations under the first four rules which their contemporaries of today would find difficult to emulate. Similarly, the surviving correspondence of many notable men and women of the nineteenth century frequently indicates a standard of letter writing, in terms of composition, style and taste, rarely matched today. On the other hand it could be argued that twentieth-century means of communication – typewriters, telephones, word processors, fax machines and the like – render such accomplishments, if not obsolete, at least of less value than they once were, given the rise of new areas of knowledge and skills.

Whether National Curriculum assessment procedures will raise standards is not yet clear. Both the longer historical perspective (from 1862) and the more immediate (from 1988) indicate that their capacity to do so will depend upon the full involvement and participation of those engaged in the day-to-day work of learning and teaching – pupils, teachers and parents – and a shared concern for formative, as well as managerial purposes.

NOTES

1. *National Commission Report*, 1993, 3.
2. *National Commission Briefings*, 1993, 135.
3. *The Times*, 28 February 1994.
4. Gipps and Stobart, 1993, 15–18.
5. Gipps and Stobart, 1993, 18.
6. *DFE News*, 11 May 1993.
7. *The Times*, 15 December 1993.
8. *The Times*, 21 November 1994.
9. *Independent*, 25 August 1994.
10. *Times Educational Supplement*, 12 July 1991.
11. *National Commission Report*, 1993, 71.
12. Montgomery, 1978, 10.
13. Chapman, 1985, 57.
14. Ball, 1983, 96–8.
15. Ball, 1983, 99.

16. Quoted in Goldstrom, 1972, 161–2.
17. Gordon and Lawton, 1978, 123.
18. Sutherland, 1984, 290.

SUGGESTED READING

Fisher, P. (1982) *External Examinations in Secondary Schools in England, 1944–1964*.
Gipps, C. and Stobart G. (1993) *Assessment: a Teachers' Guide to the Issues*.
Gordon, P. (1980) *Selection for Secondary Education*.
Montgomery, R. (1978) *A New Examination of Examinations*.
OECD (1993) *Curriculum Reform: Assessment in Question*.
Roach, J. (1971) *Public Examinations in England, 1850–1900*.
Wiseman, S. (1961) *Examinations and English Education*.

FOUR
Teaching Quality

CURRENT ISSUES

Teachers are central to education, and good quality teachers are central to good quality education. In 1983 the issue was placed firmly on the contemporary agenda with the publication of a government white paper, *Teaching Quality*. Ten years later, *Learning to Succeed*, the report of the National Commission on Education, devoted a chapter to 'Teachers and Teaching' which outlined many continuing concerns.[1] Current issues about teachers may be divided into four broad groups: recruitment and retention; effective teaching; teacher training; teacher professionalism. Concentration here will be upon teachers in schools, but many of the points apply equally to teachers in other sectors of education.

The first area of concern is that of recruitment and retention. Although, in the 1980s, it appeared that school teaching had finally become an all-graduate profession, the licensed teacher scheme of 1990 permitted the recruitment to teaching of non-graduates, albeit such teachers should have a minimum of two years of successfully completed higher education. A more radical scheme, announced in June 1993, countenanced further dilution by proposing that teachers of nursery and infant children should be recruited from 'parents and other mature students with considerable experience of working with young children'[2] but no experience whatsoever of higher education. This plan was fiercely countered, and the combined opposition of teachers and parents ensured that the 'Mums' Army' was not allowed to infiltrate the schools.

Proposals to lower the academic qualifications of prospective teachers, justified by government in terms of providing a variety of high-quality routes into teaching, reflect the fact that there has been a continuing problem in recruiting and retaining teachers. Even those who enter teaching via the traditional routes of a three- or four-year first degree in education or a one-year postgraduate course, are of lower academic ability, overall, in comparison with the cohorts of those entering and completing higher education. Given that some 30 per cent of the population is now experiencing higher education, this is a matter of considerable concern. There is particular difficulty in respect of the recruitment of secondary school teachers of such shortage subjects as mathematics and science. For example, of entrants to PGCE mathematics courses in universities in 1991, more than 30 per cent had lower second-class, and more than 20 per cent third-class degrees.[3] The status of a first degree in education is low, so that, as a result of student (and other) pressures, those taking a first degree in the subject now tend to opt for a BA or BSc (Education) rather than the basic qualification of BEd. Even more disturbing is the fact that within schools, both at primary and secondary levels, many lessons are taught by teachers who have neither qualifications nor training in respect of some of the subjects they are teaching.

As for retention, given the low morale of some teachers in England, the constant assaults upon them by governments and the press (and increasingly by pupils), the poor salary scales and career prospects for those who wish to remain in the classroom as opposed to taking on administrative duties, the increasing amount of extra-teaching duties, which now can take up more than half of a working week of between fifty and fifty-five hours, and the poor self-image of teachers themselves, there are in the 1990s almost as many qualified schoolteachers in England, at least 300,000, who are not currently teaching in schools, as those who are.

In 1995, Her Majesty's Chief Inspector of Schools, Chris Woodhead, in an article entitled 'Teach our Teachers a Lesson', declared that 'What matters ultimately is the effectiveness of teachers'.[4] Not surprisingly, given the problems of recruitment and retention, there is evidence that much of the teaching that goes on in English schools is not of good quality. The annual report of the Senior Chief Inspector for Schools, published in 1992, showed that of 22,500 sessions in 3,250 inspected primary schools in the year 1990–91, 30 per cent of lessons were considered to be poor. Of 18,000 sessions inspected in 2,400 secondary schools, 27 per cent were classified as poor.[5]

One of the central themes of this book is that many of the problems in English education today stem from a confrontational culture. Nowhere is this more evident than in the confrontation over low standards of achievement, and who is to blame. For example, in 1995 Woodhead blamed lack of teacher effectiveness upon a hostility towards didactic teaching methods, and the prevalence of unquestioned progressive orthodoxies. He commended the government's plans to reform teacher training: 'New entrants to the profession must be exposed not to dogma and rhetoric, but to teachers with the highest possible expectations of themselves and their pupils.'[6] Understandably, institutions of teacher training regret such attacks upon their professional integrity and value. Similarly, teachers themselves may both question the validity of such statistics as quoted above, and suggest that many problems should be attributed not to deficiencies in the capabilities of teachers but rather to other factors over which teachers have little or no control.

Since the 1960s research on effective teaching has centred on classroom interactions between teachers and pupils. Kyriacou has identified three major, though at times inter-related, approaches. The first focuses upon 'active learning time' (ALT), and 'quality of instruction' (QI). ALT refers to 'the amount of time spent by pupils actively engaged in the learning task and activities designed to bring about the educational outcome desired', while QI relates to 'the quality of the learning task and the activities in terms of their appropriateness and suitability in bringing about the educational outcomes desired'.[7]

The second approach places emphasis upon the psychological state of the pupil, and concentrates upon identifying the key psychological concepts, principles and processes involved in effective teaching. These include: 'attention, memory, transfer, reinforcement, mental set, cueing, feedback, concept discrimination, motivation, identification, ability, information processing, expectations, attitudes and self concept'.[8] The effective teacher is one who can recognize the psychological factors at play, and provide the appropriate responses.

The third approach defines teaching essentially as a managerial activity. Such management includes an awareness of both general teaching skills, and those appropriate to the particular discipline or area of study. The effective teacher must also bear in mind 'the appropriateness of the content, method and structure of the learning activities for the desired educational outcomes'.[9]

Effective teaching, therefore, would appear to depend upon teachers being able to organize the classroom, pupils and learning experiences appropriately, maximize active learning time and quality instruction, recognize psychological factors at play in the classroom and provide appropriate responses, and secure the desired outcomes.

Such analysis gives some indication of the complexity of the teacher's role, but of course teaching does not take place in a vacuum and a number of other factors or variables also need to be taken into account. These include 'context variables', for example the age, sex, experience, personality and social class of teacher and pupils, and such characteristics as the nature of the community, subject, class, classroom, school, time of day. Context variables can influence successful teaching to a considerable degree. For example, a teacher may be able to secure above average grades as measured by national standards for all of her pupils in one school, but have great difficulty in securing average grades for half of her pupils in another. This difference may not depend upon any change in skill or effort on the part of the teacher, but rather upon such factors as pupil ability, performance in other subjects, pupil and parental expectations, class size and resources, over which she may have very limited control.[10]

Other factors to influence effective teaching include 'process variables' which relate to teacher and pupil behaviour and interaction, and 'product variables' which relate to the desired educational outcomes. These are many and various, for example 'increased knowledge and skills; increased interest in the subject or topic; increased intellectual motivation; increased academic self-confidence and self-esteem; increased development of pupil autonomy; and increased social development'.[11]

Not only is the teacher's role highly complex; so, too, are the issues which arise from the several variables. To take one example, that of class size.

In January 1994 there were some 7.9 million pupils in 26,400 schools in England. Of these 92 per cent attended maintained schools, 7 per cent independent schools, and 1 per cent special schools. The maintained sector employed 390,400 full-time equivalent teachers, of whom 180,600 were in primary, and 178,900 in secondary schools. Independent schools employed 52,600 full-time equivalent teachers, with a further 15,900 in special schools. The overall pupil–teacher ratio in maintained schools was 18.1:1 (22.7:1 in primary and 16.4:1 in secondary) and in special schools 6.1:1. Comparable figures for January 1993 were 17.8:1 and 6.0:1. The raising of pupil–teacher ratios in maintained schools contrasted with the situation in independent schools, where the figure of 10.3:1 for January 1994 represented a slight decrease from the 10.4:1 of the previous year. Average class sizes as taught by one teacher in maintained schools also rose during the year. In January 1994 average class sizes stood at 26.9 in primary and 21.4 in secondary schools. Average hours of lesson time for pupils in Key Stage 1 and 2 were 23.1; and in Key Stages 3 and 4, 24.6.[12]

Table 4.1: Average size of classes taught by one teacher in maintained schools in England, 1990–94

	1990	1991	1992	1993	1994
Primary	25.9	26.3	26.4	26.6	26.9
Secondary	20.3	20.6	20.9	21.2	21.4

The percentage of classes with more than 30 pupils also steadily increased over the same period: in maintained primary schools from 17.5 to 21.4, and in secondary from 4.0 to 5.2.[13]

Comparative data from OECD demonstrates that whereas class size in English secondary schools is close to average, class size in primary schools is high. While most countries (in common with England) have higher class sizes in secondary than in primary schools, in the Netherlands, New Zealand and Sweden this situation is reversed.[14]

Three obvious conclusions can be drawn from these statistics. The first is that class sizes in maintained primary schools are considerably larger than those in maintained secondary schools. The second, that class sizes in maintained schools have steadily increased in recent years and, given the latest round of funding announced for education in January 1995, will continue to do so. The figures also demonstrate that class size is one of the most distinctive differences between maintained and independent schools.

Although 'commonsense', the commitment of independent school head teachers, teachers and parents, and several research studies from the USA suggest that pupils achieve more in smaller classes, unanimity on this point does not prevail. Optimum class sizes may vary according to the age and abilities of children and to the subjects being taught. Another important factor is that of teaching methods, which must be appropriate to the size of group.

The two final issues identified in the first paragraph of this chapter, teacher training and teacher professionalism, have also been matters of considerable controversy. The education and training of teachers should include not only initial preparation, but also schemes for induction into teaching and subsequent regular opportunities for in-service study. In recent years government policy has been to diminish the influence and role of higher education institutions in the education and training of teachers, and to increase those of government and schools. Another concern has been to diminish the influence and role of teacher unions in a variety of issues, most notably in the area of teachers' pay and conditions, but nevertheless to deny to English teachers what their counterparts in Scotland have enjoyed since 1966 – a General Teaching Council. These issues will be dealt with in more detail in the next section which will be divided into three parts: a good teacher; teacher education and training; teacher professionalism.

HISTORICAL PERSPECTIVES

A good teacher

In the 1990s there is general agreement about the qualities of a good teacher. It is widely believed that good teachers are 'keen and enthusiastic, firm but fair, stimulating, know their stuff and are interested in the welfare of their students', and 'few would attempt to defend the converse: that good teachers are unenthusiastic, boring, unfair, ignorant and do not care about their pupils'.[15]

Many of these characteristics have been identified and approved across the centuries. John Locke's *Some Thoughts Concerning Education* (1693), provides much good information and sound common sense on teaching qualities and methods. Although Locke was writing in the context of the tutoring of an individual pupil, rather than a school classroom, his own experience of teaching, coupled with his expertise as a doctor and as a pioneer of psychology, ensured that the *Thoughts* contain many maxims which are as appropriate today as they were in the seventeenth century: for example, 'Praise in public; blame in private'.

In 1707, in a book entitled *The Christian Schoolmaster*, the Revd James Talbott, rector of Spofforth in Yorkshire, outlined the personality traits and skills which he believed a prospective schoolmaster should possess to be effective in the teaching of the children of the poor. This work was commissioned by the Society for Promoting Christian Knowledge, a body established at the end of the seventeenth century and prominent in the promotion of charity schools, as a means of promoting the effectiveness of schoolteachers

As the title of Talbott's book indicated, he was writing about male teachers who were to be good Christians. He also favoured recruiting teachers from among those aged 25 or over, and of 'normal' physical features. He emphasised the importance of competence in the subjects to be taught – the principles of the Christian religion, reading, writing and arithmetic. Training in the methods of teaching (there were no teacher training colleges at this time) was to be at the hands of a more experienced master already working at the school. 'Patience and humility' were required, so that the teacher could work calmly and conscientiously with his pupils – at their level and at their pace. Talbott argued, indeed, that the learning activity should proceed 'as the age and understanding of children will admit'.[16] 'Sagacity and judgement' were required, so that the teacher might recognize 'the particular disposition and temper of those he is to teach, and may suit his instructions and admonitions accordingly'.[17] 'Justice and equity' were important for the impartial distribution of rewards and punishment, while 'meekness and forbearance' were important for moderation when it came to discipline. Talbott, indeed, believed in the efficacy of rewards – commendation and advancement – as a means of controlling children. Where punishment was necessary this should first be in the form of reproof or demotion, with only exceptional recourse to corporal punishment or expulsion. He advocated 'Candour and sweetness of disposition' in order that the teacher might 'gain the affections, and consequently the attention of those he teaches; it being almost as natural for every one to learn from those he loves, as 'tis to learn what he loves'.[18] 'Diligence and application' were necessary for the close and constant attention to the teacher's many duties, but the most important quality of all was a 'pious and devout frame of spirit'.

In the nineteenth century James Kay-Shuttleworth, first secretary to the Committee of the Privy Council on Education, established in 1839, identified similar personality traits and skills as being essential to good teaching. For Kay-Shuttleworth, Christian devotion, humility and industriousness were prime qualities to be sought, and developed, in the teachers of the poor. He also, like Talbott, emphasised the importance of pedagogical skills, for example the ability to teach in accordance with the pupils' understanding, and to engage their interest, so that 'to learn is no longer a task but a pleasure'.[19] Effective teachers would be imbued with:

> habits of thought and demeanour so disciplined as to enable them to sustain a moral dignity while they mingle with the sports, sympathize with the feelings, yet elevate the thoughts of children – capable of making knowledge attractive by the simplicity and kindness with which it is imparted – imbued with a deep sense of their religious responsibilities; and hallowing all their moral instruction by a constant reference to the sanctions of religion.[20]

Two conclusions may be drawn from these examples. The first is that many of the qualities, personality traits and attitudes advocated by such educationists as Locke, Talbott and Kay-Shuttleworth as typical of a good teacher, are consistent with those identified by Wragg. Their writings are also consistent with elements of effective teaching noted by Kyriacou – for example key psychological concepts, principles and processes. Two other approaches to effective teaching identified by Kyriacou, those of active learning time and classroom management, were also very evident in nineteenth-century manuals on teaching methods.

But if there are similarities, there are also differences. One difference concerns a change in the desired outcomes of mass schooling. The promotion of the Christian faith and the rescue of the children of the poor are no longer the prime purposes of education, as they were in the charity and elementary schools of the eighteenth and early nineteenth centuries. From the second half of the nineteenth century teachers were characterized by (indeed at times caricatured for) their possession of a substantial amount of secular knowledge. In consequence less emphasis is placed today upon the Christian and moral dimensions of the teacher, as of the pupils. Another significant difference, which is also connected in large part to the issue of Christianity, is that in the eighteenth and early nineteenth centuries, teachers in charity and elementary schools were predominantly male. By the end of the nineteenth century the majority of teachers in such schools were female.

One final point to be noted here concerns the issue of recruitment and retention. While Talbott, Kay-Shuttleworth and others might set forth the noblest ideals, both of teachers and of teaching, as Kay-Shuttleworth himself admitted,

> in many cases, the profession of the educator has fallen into the hands of persons who are destitute of means, not merely from want of ability, but from defects of character, and who resort to this calling after they have been proved to be unfit for any other.[21]

Teacher education and training

Training, like indoctrination, may be defined as a process of instruction whereby information, procedures and values are conveyed to another person, with little or no room for question or amendment. Education may be considered to be a larger process, one which enables the recipient to engage in the process of instruction, to modify or even to control the agenda, and to reach different conclusions from the educator. One indication of the distinction is the existence of the term 'self-educated', for it would be uncommon to state that a person could be self-trained. The term 'teacher education' may be used to describe both the education of teachers in a subject – for example, history or music – that they are to teach or study for their own personal development, and in the process of teaching itself. Historically speaking, however, the term 'teacher training' has predominated. It was widely used in the nineteenth century, and although in the 1960s the redesignation of teacher training colleges as colleges of education, and the introduction of the Bachelor of Education degree, gave priority to the term 'education', training is now re-established. Teacher training is now used officially by central government, for example with the establishment in 1994 of a Teacher Training Agency.

Four broad approaches to teacher education and training may be identified, both in an historical and in a conceptual sense. These may be called: apprenticeship; teacher training; teacher education; and partnership.

Apprenticeship implies training rather than education. The apprentice learns a skill from a master or mistress – learning by doing, without question or amendment. The monitorial, or mutual, system of instruction, was developed independently in the last decade of the eighteenth century by the Quaker, Joseph Lancaster, at Borough Road in Southwark, and by the Anglican clergyman, Andrew Bell, in Madras in India. In 1797 Bell returned to England, where his principles of instruction, both of teachers and of pupils, were taken up by the National Society, founded in 1811. In 1814 the British and Foreign School Society replaced the Royal Lancasterian Institution, set up in 1808 to promote Lancaster's work. These two societies not only provided a considerable number of nineteenth-century elementary schools, and were recipients of government grants for education from 1833, they also began the work of training teachers. Borough Road is generally counted as the first modern teacher training institution in England; subsequently, however, the great majority of English teacher training colleges were associated with the National Society and the Anglican church. The monitorial system necessitated two levels of training. The first was the training of the monitors by the master; the second the training of further masters, and subsequently mistresses, in how to operate the system. Since few teachers could afford the time or expense to receive a formal course of training in London, both societies also produced teacher manuals and textbooks.

Both Lancaster and Bell made great claims for their systems and for the power they would give to teachers. Lancaster believed that one teacher, seated in a large school room and instructing the monitors in their duties, could supervise one thousand children. Not to be outdone, Bell claimed that one teacher could oversee ten thousand children. Naturally, the training of teachers to perform such wonders was strongly supported. Some argued, indeed, that the monitorial system was more important than the steam engine in its capacity to diminish the labour of the teacher and to multiply work on behalf of the pupil. Lancaster placed great emphasis upon the efficient use of time, and in *Improvements in Education* (1806), he set out, in minute detail, the roles of monitors and tutors, the principles of small group teaching, the use of drill, repetition and practice, the employment of co-operation and competition, and the nature and use of a variety of rewards and punishments.

Although the monitorial system of instruction was even employed in some English public schools, and spread to many parts of the globe, by the 1830s its effectiveness was being questioned. For example, Kay-Shuttleworth argued that

> such acquirements as are made in these schools result almost solely from an effort of the memory which receives a meagre supply of the most rudimentary knowledge, while in a great number, if not the majority of instances, as this knowledge is received with distaste, it is not retained long after the children leave school . . . [22]

Monitors, therefore, declined in numbers, and were replaced by a new breed of trainees – the pupil teacher apprentices. In 1846 the government established a formal apprenticeship system whereby able children would be bound to a five-year apprenticeship, usually between the ages of 13 and 18. During the day they taught in the school; in the evening they received further instruction in subjects and methods of teaching from the teacher. They also had to submit to an annual inspection by one of Her Majesty's Inspectors. For this arduous existence they were paid on a scale rising in equal increments from £10 to £20 per annum. Teachers in charge of pupil teachers received £5 per annum for the first, £4 for the second and £3 for any additional ones. At the end of their apprenticeship pupil teachers might either progress to a training college, with the financial assistance of a Queen's Scholarship of some £20 or £25 per annum and thus qualify as a certificated teacher, proceed directly into uncertificated teaching, or leave teaching altogether.

Pupil teachers were popular with school managers, as they were cheaper to employ than 'proper' teachers, and by 1861, when the Newcastle Commission reported, there were some 13,871 in schools in England and Wales.[23] Numbers fell under the Revised Code of 1862, which abolished both the fixed rates of pupil teachers' pay and the augmentation of the salaries of those teachers who taught them. With the advent of the Elementary Education Act of 1870 pupil teachers were in great demand. Numbers doubled, from 14,612 to 32,128, while the numbers of certificated teachers increased from 12,467 to 31,422.[24] The first decade of the twentieth century saw an even more dramatic decline. In 1900 there were still 30,783 pupil teachers, nearly one-quarter of the teaching force in elementary schools. By 1913–14 there were only 1,691.[25] One cause of this decline was the development of maintained secondary schools, which meant that it was no longer necessary to bind young people to teaching at an early age. In 1907 a bursary scheme was introduced which enabled intending teachers to attend secondary schools. Holders of bursaries were still able to spend a year in an elementary school as a student teacher before proceeding to college. Within three years bursars outnumbered pupil teachers.

Meanwhile the teacher training colleges flourished apace. In the second decade of the nineteenth century there were only two: Borough Road and the National Society's training institution at Baldwin's Gardens off the Gray's Inn Road in London. Diocesan training institutions multiplied from the 1830s, so that by 1860 there were thirty-four colleges, and by 1890, forty-three. Nevertheless, even in 1900 only a quarter of those teaching in elementary schools in England had been college trained. One reason for this was that during the nineteenth century teacher training remained firmly under voluntary control. Only in the last decade of the nineteenth century, with the advent of day training colleges associated with the universities, and the establishment of local education authority training colleges following the Education Act of 1902, was the situation changed.

By the middle of the nineteenth century three broad approaches to teacher training and the concept of the good teacher had emerged. The first, and the most enduring, was that promoted by Kay-Shuttleworth in his college at Battersea – that of service, humility and attention to the basics. Battersea, begun in 1840 as a private venture, was soon to be handed over to the National Society. A second approach found expression at another National Society college, St Mark's, Chelsea, founded in 1841. Here, under the inspired leadership of a former grammar school master, Derwent Coleridge, teacher training shaded into teacher education. Latin was the principal subject of study, and much emphasis was placed upon choral music and worship. For two of their three years of study, indeed, students concentrated upon their own education, and Coleridge, himself a renowned scholar and linguist, encouraged his students to aspire to great things. Students from St Mark's proceeded to teach in a variety of schools, and some entered the priesthood.

A third approach was that of Chester College, founded by the Chester Diocesan Board in 1840, with Arthur Rigg (like Coleridge, a Cambridge graduate) as its first Principal. Rigg was a mathematician with a firm commitment to science, laboratories and practical work. His vision was of teachers recruited from industrial and commercial backgrounds, trained in a practical and scientific environment, and carrying forward this ethos into a variety of elementary and middle-class schools.

The Revised Code of 1862, and the government-directed reform of the teacher training syllabus which preceded it, ensured the victory of the Battersea model over those of St Mark's and Chester. Teacher training predominated over teacher education, both in respect of subjects studied and of teaching methods.

The master or mistress of method was the embodiment of good classroom practice. There was no single formula, but much drawing upon experience and discussion of the methods of such continental reformers as Herbart, Pestalozzi and Froebel. Herbart's five steps provided an essential basis to many method courses and were soundly learned and rigorously applied. These involved:

Preparation – including ascertaining the pupils' previous knowledge of the subject;

Presentation – of the new knowledge by the teacher;

Association – of new material with existing knowledge;

Condensation – a reflective stage when old and new knowledge were united into a coherent whole;

Application – the use and testing of the new knowledge.[26]

Teacher education, in the sense of the development of education as a discipline, began in England with the lectures of Joseph Payne, the first Professor of Education in England, at the College of Preceptors in 1873. The great majority of those who attended his courses were women teachers in secondary schools who, as yet, had scant access to university degrees. In 1890, following the final report of the Cross Commission, the government gave formal approval to the establishment of day training institutions in universities and university colleges. Students in such institutions (residential facilities were soon established, making the original day training concept obsolete) had access to other lectures of the university and were able to take degrees. Although the prime purpose was still to train teachers for elementary schools, a variety of routes developed. One-year courses for graduates existed alongside two- and three-year courses – subsequently extended to four years for those who intended both to graduate and to qualify as teachers. Chairs in education were established, and in the early years many of these were occupied by historians of education, study of the history of education being prescribed by government. The twentieth century saw an increasing number of professorial appointments of psychologists.

After the Second World War, more emphasis was placed upon philosophical, sociological and comparative approaches. By this time university departments of education were increasingly identified with providing one-year postgraduate courses for those intending to teach in secondary schools. Where such teachers were intended for posts in secondary grammar and independent schools, in which teaching methods were considered to be traditional and time-honoured, and pupils followed an academic curriculum, teacher education – the study of educational theory prior to educational practice – was considered to be appropriate. By the 1970s and 1980s, however, the one-year PGCE was being used as a means of preparation for teaching in primary and secondary comprehensive schools. In 1980 it became the majority route, and continued to be so. For example, in 1989 10,088 students were admitted to BEd courses and 10,460 to PGCE in England and Wales. Of the PGCE students, 6,380 were preparing for secondary, and 4,080 for primary, schools.[27] Whereas in the four-year BEd degree there might still be time for study of education in subjects, and education in respect of teaching, it was widely argued that during a one-year postgraduate course the main focus of studies should be upon the immediate tasks that teachers would be required to perform in the classroom. The relevance in initial training of the study of such 'foundation' disciplines as the history, philosophy and sociology of education was called into question.

Partnership became the watchword of the 1980s, a partnership between education and training in the preparation of teachers, and a partnership between institutions of higher education and schools. One basis for this partnership was the prominence of a new concept, that of the 'reflective practitioner', embodied in a book of that title written by Donald Schön in 1983. According to this approach students should spend much of their time practising teaching in schools, but should also be provided with substantial opportunities to reflect upon that practice. In 1984 the government appointed a Council for the Accreditation of Teacher Education (CATE) which established criteria that had to be met before courses of teacher preparation would be approved. The main thrust of CATE criteria and of subsequent government pronouncements was to increase the practitioner, as opposed to the reflective, elements. They also required schoolteachers to be fully involved in the process of education and training, not just during teaching practices but also in the selection of students and their assessment. As schools began to receive an increasing percentage of the money allotted for the initial preparation of teachers, the balance of the partnership shifted dramatically; so, too, did the location. In 1994 students on secondary PGCE courses were required to spend twenty-four of the thirty-six weeks in schools.

Four government initiatives of the 1990s confirmed the move away from partnership towards training, even apprenticeship. The articled teachers scheme, begun in 1990, provided for a two-year postgraduate initial training with students spending 80 per cent of their time in schools. The licensed teachers scheme, also begun in 1990, allowed those qualified by two years of higher education, with basic standards in maths and English, and aged 26 (subsequently reduced to 24) to teach in schools under licence. One purpose of the licensed teacher scheme was to enable schools, particularly in the London area, that were finding difficulty in recruiting teachers of such shortage subjects as mathematics, modern languages, science, and technology to fill these places. In many cases the only alternative for schools to recruiting a licensed teacher was to leave such places vacant. Though licensed teachers were supposed to be given mentors, and other forms of training, an OFSTED report of 1993 concluded that the quality of such provision was frequently poor.

The third proposal for on-the-job training, that of the 'Mums' Army' announced in 1993, was never implemented, but another initiative of that year, school-based training, has taken clear hold. Under this scheme schools assumed full control of the initial training of teachers, though they might also purchase some services from higher education institutions if they wished to do so. From 1994 schools were permitted to train teachers without any reference to institutions of higher education, and without any need for those students to acquire a university validated qualification. In 1994–95 some 450 students were being trained in schools.

Teacher professionalism

Although there is no absolute definition of a profession, certain general characteristics of occupations generally designated as professions may be identified. Professions are usually concerned with a defined area of knowledge, while entry to them requires a specialized training and the possession of a universally recognized qualification. Some professions maintain a separate code of ethics, over and above the law of the land, which governs relationships between members of the profession and their clients. Finally, professions have their own controlling body, a body which exercises responsibility for the areas of knowledge, training, certification and the ethical code.

Classic professions in English history have been those based upon the Church, medicine and the law. Teachers, however, have had considerable difficulty in approximating to the professional model. There is no clearly defined area of specialist (or esoteric) knowledge. Although specialized training and recognized qualifications exist, and although, from the 1980s, teaching achieved the status of an all-graduate occupation, developments since that date have reversed the position. One reason for the inability of teachers to maintain their status is the lack of a controlling body, unlike Scotland where a General Teaching Council was created under legislation of 1965. Another difficulty for teachers has been that of image. Members of traditional professions have largely been comfortable middle-class males, the majority of whose clients are adults. They are exempt from direct government controls and have little or no recourse to strikes.

Two other characteristics of teachers have been their considerable numbers and many divisions. In the medieval period the degree of MA was in effect a licence to teach, either in grammar schools or in the universities. Indeed, the university degree remained the basic qualification for teachers in grammar schools until well into the twentieth century: no further qualification was deemed to be necessary. Although, in the early modern period, many young graduates took posts as tutors or as schoolmasters while on their way to more lucrative employment in Church or state, the master of a grammar school was considered to have a freehold in his office, while the founders and owners of private schools and academies could run these as a profitable business, like any other. At the other end of the scale, however, some teachers of schools for the poor were those who could do little or nothing else. Some took to teaching as a result of physical incapacity – including those unfit for manual work, and maimed ex-soldiers and seamen. Others combined teaching with a second occupation, cobbling or tailoring, taking in washing or mending.

These divisions (and connections) continued into the nineteenth century. Headmasters of boys' public schools might have considerable influence and substantial salaries. Their status would be on a par with that of the master of an Oxford or Cambridge college or of a bishop. Indeed these worlds were closely linked, and some Victorian headmasters, for example Benson and Temple, even became Archbishops of Canterbury. Such men were as far removed as could be from the teachers in private working-class and elementary schools. These teachers, both men and women, were not only poor: they also lacked the academic status accorded to primary school teachers in many other European countries, including Scotland. Their education, in school, as pupil teachers, even in the training colleges, was essentially elementary. Between these teachers and the graduate HMI who inspected them a great gulf was fixed. One crucial element in this was the pupil teacher. Kay-Shuttleworth intended that all pupil teachers would proceed to a training college, and that schools would be staffed by trained, certificated teachers, but that goal was not achieved. Though certification was permitted without college training, during the nineteenth century most teachers were unqualified. The most significant feature of the teaching force of the second half of the nineteenth century was not the trained certificated teacher, but the pupil teacher to whom, from the age of 13, the education of children of the poor was entrusted by governments and school managers alike.

The Minute of 1846, which established the system of pupil teachers, provided extra grants to teachers who supervised their work, scholarships and grants to training colleges and a system of teachers' certificates. It also guaranteed supplementation of the salaries of teachers who had undergone training and whose schools received a government grant, on the condition that the school provided a rent-free house and a salary equal to at least twice the government supplementation. Since the maximum supplementation for a three-year trained teacher was £30 per annum, such a teacher might be assured of a minimum salary of £90 plus accommodation: a modest, but nevertheless welcome competence. Such guaranteed augmentation, together with the prospect of a pension scheme, appeared to suggest that teachers were on the road to becoming government employees, civil servants indeed. It promised a considerable change from the days when the parish schoolmaster, as described by Talbott, also fulfilled such duties as parish clerk, surveyor and rate collector, as a means of supplementing his meagre income.

The Revised Code of 1862 shattered such pretensions. Those who controlled the Education Department, both politicians and administrators, expressed alarm that the training colleges were creating a breed of men and women who considered themselves to be superior, both to the humble origins from which most of them had sprung, and to the necessary drudgery of teaching the basic subjects. Direct payments to certificated teachers and pupil teachers were abolished. In future all grants would be made to managers, who would determine salaries for teachers and pupil teachers. Contracts with the latter would be reduced to six months, while the salaries of teachers would depend to a great extent upon the success (or failure) of their pupils in the annual examinations. The brief glimmerings of improved security and status were extinguished. Pupil teacher numbers fell dramatically. The plight of the training colleges was even worse. Government grants for buildings and improvements were discontinued. Some colleges closed altogether; others survived only by lowering their standards and taking in all who could afford to pay for their courses. Candidates applying for training colleges fell from 2,513 in 1862 to 1,584 in 1866.[28] At Chester student numbers fell to five, and Rigg resigned in despair.

At Chester, as elsewhere, however, the demand for teachers occasioned by the

Elementary Education Act of 1870 led to a swift reversal of fortune. Some of the new school boards offered the prospect of a genuine career once more, and one not subject to the whims of managers or parsons. But although numbers of pupil teachers and students in training colleges began to increase, the laws of supply and demand ensured that many schools were forced to take on unqualified teachers. In 1898 more than half the female teachers and some 30 per cent of male teachers in public elementary schools were untrained. These percentages were considerably higher than in 1875.[29]

In the twentieth century most teachers became employees of the local education authorities. From 1944 they experienced considerable freedom in such matters as curriculum, teaching methods and the exercise of discipline. Since the 1980s such freedom has been curtailed by legislation, while the powers of local education authorities, themselves, have been severely limited.

Divisions between teachers, which reflected the divisions of nineteenth-century English society and its schools, were mirrored by decisions of teachers themselves, and perpetuated long after the rationale for such divisions had largely disappeared. The oldest surviving teachers' association is the College of Preceptors, founded in 1846 by a group of private schoolteachers, and granted a royal charter in 1849. The National Union of Elementary Teachers (NUET, now NUT) was formed in 1870, the union for those employed in elementary schools, as distinct from the four associations of masters, mistresses, headmasters and headmistresses created between 1874 and 1891 (later known as the Joint Four) to represent the interests of those in secondary grammar schools. The distinctions in the very titles, between teacher and union on the one hand and master and mistress and association on the other, spoke volumes. Even more 'superior' were the headmasters of the boys' public schools who banded together in the Headmasters' Conference.

Early in the twentieth century there were two breakaway movements from the NUT. The Union of Women Teachers (UWT) seceded to promote the issue of equal pay for women; the National Association of Schoolmasters (NAS) to safeguard the interests of the male career teacher. In 1970 the Professional Association of Teachers (PAT) was formed by teachers who were opposed to strike action under any circumstances. Though today the names have changed – the NAS is now the NAS/UWT, and the Joint Four have become the Association of Teachers and Lecturers (ATL) – and though the identification of groups of teachers with particular associations has been blurred, for example many primary teachers left the NUT in the 1970s and 1980s, teachers are still thoroughly divided. Membership figures in 1993 were: NUT, 182,644; NAS/UWT, 138,381; ATL, 136,645; PAT, 40,223. This situation contrasts strongly with Scotland, where nearly all teachers are members of the Educational Institute of Scotland (EIS).

During the second half of the nineteenth century the College of Preceptors was to the fore in promoting the idea of a General Teaching Council by means of a Scholastic Registration Act, similar to the General Medical Council established in 1860. But though a Teachers' Registration Council was brought into being in 1902 its nature was divisive, while the Royal Society of Teachers, created in 1929, died a lingering death some twenty years later. Since 1965, when a General Teaching

Council was established for Scotland by statute, there have been a series of initiatives to secure a similar body for England and Wales.

During the 1980s and 1990s teachers' control of their own destinies further declined. After a series of strikes in the mid-1980s they were deprived of the traditional pay bargaining machinery, the Burnham Committee, established in 1919, and minimum hours of work were laid down by government. The National Curriculum, and its associated testing, has removed much of their freedom of action within the classroom, although teachers' protests have secured some modifications in the original requirements.

CONCLUSION

Conclusions about teachers may be drawn in respect of the four areas outlined under current issues: recruitment and retention; effective teaching; teacher training; and teacher professionalism.

The historical perspective shows that while teachers in some schools have always been recruited from amongst the ablest graduates, teachers in other schools have been of very low calibre indeed. In the nineteenth century the pupil teacher scheme was in many senses a substitute (and a poor one at that) for secondary schooling. In the nineteenth century some training colleges were virtually obliged to take in any candidates who had the necessary financial support; and in the twentieth, the intellectual level of many of those who attended training colleges continued to be low. Even after the Second World War, some entrants had no post-16 qualifications, so that the academic level of some teacher training institutions was closer to that of a school sixth form than of a university.

Naturally, at certain times, for example in the aftermath of the Education Act of 1870, or following the Second World War, there were great shortages of teachers and recourse was made to extreme measures. For example, between 1944 and 1951 some 35,000 ex-servicemen and women were trained under emergency schemes, some of only one term's duration. But the historical perspective would suggest that the root problem of recruitment of teachers lies in the low standards and status of teachers in nineteenth-century elementary schools which were transmitted into many of the primary and secondary modern schools of the twentieth century.

The problem of retention also betrays its historic roots. Although the initial salaries of teachers have, on occasion, not been substantially different from those entering other occupations, their opportunities for advancement in a financial sense, particularly while remaining as classroom teachers, have been poor in the extreme. The major avenue of promotion has been out of the classroom into administrative roles, either within schools or in other parts of the education service. This situation has had a very long history indeed, and reflects the worth placed by society upon the classroom teacher. In 1581 Richard Mulcaster posed the question which still merits an answer some 400 years later, 'Why should not teachers be well provided for, to continue their whole life in the schoole, as Divines, Lawyers, Physicians do in their several professions?'[30]

Issues of recruitment and retention bear heavily upon that of effective teaching.

If teachers' expectations of children in many schools are too low, that is in part because society's expectations of teachers have also been too low. Were teachers to be recruited from amongst the best, rather than the worst of entrants to, and graduates from, higher education, were they to undergo a much longer period of training and induction and their performance to be subject to more regular and rigorous scrutiny, and were they to be accorded the remuneration and status commensurate with these enhanced qualifications, training and responsibilities, problems of recruitment and retention would be substantially solved.

Effective teaching would also be promoted by such measures. Teaching, as the survey by Kyriacou quoted in the first section of this chapter admirably demonstrates, is a most complex and challenging occupation, not least because it takes place with reference to children (for whom the teacher stands *in loco parentis*) rather than to adults. Progress in effective teaching will be made when such improvements in teacher training and competence on the one hand, and school buildings and class sizes on the other, are seen as complementary parts of a reform package, rather than being used as ammunition in an ideological debate.

Effective teaching naturally depends not only upon the recruitment and retention of persons of high quality, it also requires high quality initial education and training, induction, and in-service support. Unfortunately, the cost of such provision is considerable and, as the historical record shows, the proper preparation of teachers has frequently been sacrificed to financial expediency. Pupil teachers were employed because they cost less than adult teachers.

One-year postgraduate training for teachers has mushroomed in part because it is cheaper than a four-year degree route, even though one year is manifestly inadequate for the preparation of teachers in primary schools. Similarly, there is a danger that school-based training will mean a reversion to the employment of low-cost apprentices, with students substituting for qualified teachers. Another contemporary proposal, which also has strong historical antecedents, is that of using classroom assistants in support of teachers. Such assistants might undertake many of the non-professional duties which currently occupy much of a teacher's time, but also might be used as a means of justifying increases in class sizes.

There may be no single best route into teaching, but certain elements would appear to be essential in the initial and subsequent education and training of teachers. The first point to make is that both education and training are required. Teachers should be educated persons, and recognizable as such, not least in respect of education. Some, if not all, of that education should take place in institutions of higher education. On many occasions in the nineteenth and twentieth centuries education in education has been dismissed as 'mere' theory or ideology, a process which seems to have accelerated since 1984. But it is only initial and subsequent engagement with the intellectual discipline of education that will enable teachers (and others) to avoid subservience to half-understood and ill-digested theories, and educational ideology – from whatever quarter. Some elements of pedagogy, both those that are general and others with specific subject application, may also be introduced most effectively in a higher-education environment. The historical perspective demonstrates the importance of the higher-education element in teacher education since the 1890s.

At a time when other professions in England are strengthening their links with higher education, when courses of teacher preparation in other countries are being lengthened and located within the university sector, policies to separate teacher education from higher education, or indeed to eliminate teacher education altogether, must be called into question.

On the other hand, training, which may include elements of apprenticeship, should take place in schools. Many elements of teaching are clearly best learned on the job under the eye of a skilled practitioner. But apprenticeship, on its own, is insufficient. Students need to generalize from their specific situations. They need to reflect upon their experiences with students, teachers and tutors from schools other than those in which they are practising.

In the 1990s central government has promoted training (and apprenticeship) over education, and located such training in the schools. Such reforms may produce more effective teachers. However, the historical perspective suggests that such schemes may also be designed essentially to reduce costs, by employing students in place of qualified practitioners, and thereby saving money both in schools and in higher education. The balancing of budgets and the saving of public money are laudable ends in themselves. Nevertheless, it is clear that while apprenticeship may be a proper route into some manual (and other forms) of employment, on its own it is an inadequate preparation for entry into a profession. It is also possible that school-based training, if properly executed, will be more expensive than the system it replaces.

There are two views about professions. On the one hand they may be seen as groups motivated by the highest ideals, dedicated to the service of the public. On the other they may be interpreted as bodies designed to corner a market and raise the price of goods and services. Since 1979 Conservative governments have taken the latter view and have sought, with considerable success, to weaken the powers of trade unions and of some professions. Conservative analysis of education has been based upon the premise that the system was dominated by producers, to the disadvantage of consumers; as a consequence the powers and rights of teachers, as represented through their associations and unions, have been severely diminished. Government influence has been exercised through such quangos as the Council for the Accreditation of Teacher Education, the School Curriculum and Assessment Authority and the Teacher Training Agency.

Whatever the faults of the teacher associations and unions, however, the necessity of modifying recent reforms in such areas as the National Curriculum and national testing shows the great danger of political, as opposed to professional, direction of education. Some government interventions, for example prescribing minimum hours of work, have had exactly the opposite effect to that intended. Similarly, the failure to consider seriously the comments of teachers about the difficulties of implementing a national curriculum and national testing has retarded, rather than advanced, the effectiveness of such measures. The contrast with Scotland, where the existence of a General Teaching Council has ensured that discussions have been of a professional and constructive, rather than of an ideological and confrontational nature, has been instructive. This contrast reflects the quite different position, in terms of status and role in the national culture and consciousness, that Scottish teachers have enjoyed. If good quality teachers are, indeed, central to good quality education, there is much to be learned from the Scottish example.

NOTES

1. *National Commission Report*, 1993, 193–237.
2. *DFE News*, 188/93.
3. *National Commission Report*, 1993, 204.
4. *The Times*, 26 January 1995.
5. *National Commission Report*, 1993, 204.
6. *The Times*, 26 January 1995.
7. Kyriacou, 1992, 25.
8. Kyriacou, 1992, 29.
9. Kyriacou, 1992, 31.
10. Kyriacou, 1992, 9–10.
11. Kyriacou, 1992, 11.
12. *DFE News*, 204/94.
13. *DFE News*, 204/94.
14. *National Commission Briefings*, 1993, 176.
15. Wragg, 1984, 4.
16. Talbott, 1707, 19.
17. Talbott, 1707, 19.
18. Talbott, 1707, 20.
19. Kay-Shuttleworth, 1839, 64.
20. Kay-Shuttleworth, 1839, 67–8.
21. Kay-Shuttleworth, 1839, 61–2.
22. Kay-Shuttleworth, 1839, 9.
23. Jones, 1924, 190.
24. Dent, 1977, 26.
25. Dent, 1977, 47, 55.
26. Castle, 1970, 140.
27. Naish, 1990, 26.
28. Rich, 1972, 186.
29. Aldrich, 1982, 56.
30. Quoted in Castle, 1970, 92.

SUGGESTED READING

Barber, M. (1992) *Education and the Teacher Unions.*
Dent, H. C. (1977) *The Training of Teachers in England and Wales, 1800–1975.*
Gordon, P. (ed.) (1983) *Is Teaching a Profession?*
Gosden, P. H. J. H. (1969) *How They Were Taught.*

Graves, N. (ed.) (1990) *Initial Teacher Education.*

Kyriacou, C. (1992) *Effective Teaching in Schools.*

Rich, R.W. (1972) *The Training of Teachers in England and Wales during the Nineteenth Century.*

Tropp, A. (1957) *The School Teachers.*

FIVE

Control

CURRENT ISSUES

The control of education has been an issue throughout history.

> For whoever exercises the supreme power in school affairs can determine educational thought and practice; and although this power may be shared or it may be united, it is as true of a school as it is of any other community that somewhere this governing authority must exist.[1]

Current issues are focused upon changes in control that have emanated from government policies since 1979. Those changes may be summarized as giving more powers to central government and to 'Quasi Autonomous Non-Governmental Organizations' (Quangos). Such powers are visible in the spheres of curriculum, assessment and teacher training. More powers have also been given to the governing bodies of schools and to head teachers, through the policies of local school management and of grant-maintained status. Those whose powers have been diminished include the local education authorities, the teachers' unions, and the teacher training institutions. The Inner London Education Authority (ILEA), the largest local education authority, was simply abolished. Some schools opted out of local education authority control, while all polytechnics and colleges were removed from their charge. Teachers' bargaining rights, as established under the Burnham Committee of 1919, were abolished. Teacher training was brought under the control of the Council for the Accreditation of Teacher Education (CATE) and subsequently of the Teacher Training Agency (TTA). The inspectorate (HMI) was recast as the Office for Standards in Education (OFSTED).

Two characteristics of these changes are immediately apparent. The first is their great extent and rapidity. The spate of educational legislation that has ensued since 1979 is quite unprecedented in English history: almost each year has seen yet another major act. The second, which is to a large extent a consequence of the first, is the confused, and at times apparently contradictory, nature of some of the changes. This confusion stems from a number of causes, ranging from personalities to ideologies.

Margaret Thatcher's tenure of the position of Secretary of State for Education from 1970 to 1974 not only gave her a particular interest in this area, but also showed her that central government's powers were severely circumscribed – she was unable, for example, to halt the spread of comprehensive reorganization of secondary schools. The hostility of the education world was apparent when subsequently, as Prime Minster, she was dealt a particularly unpleasant blow by the refusal of her Alma Mater, the University of Oxford, to grant her an honorary degree. Since 1979 there has been a succession of Secretaries of State: Mark Carlisle, Keith Joseph, Kenneth Baker, John MacGregor, Kenneth Clarke, John Patten and Gillian Shephard. Changes in personnel have led to changes in policy, but perhaps the most significant feature of this list is the high status and profile of three ministers – Joseph, Baker and Clarke – an indication of the importance that has been attached to the control and reform of education in recent years.

One of the most obvious examples of confusion and contradiction over matters of control has been that of the curriculum. The logical policy for a government committed to the operation of the market and to consumer choice would appear to be to leave the curriculum to be decided by the operation of such forces. Schools and other educational institutions should respond to the market by supplying those courses for which there is most demand. Keith Joseph, the apostle of the free market in whom Margaret Thatcher placed great trust, consistently declared himself to be against a centrally controlled national curriculum, voicing his doubts even during the passage of the Education Reform Bill through the House of Lords, as did his predecessor, Mark Carlisle. Nevertheless, by 1987 a belief in the possibility of the unfettered operation of market forces within the sphere of education was fast diminishing. Keith Joseph, Secretary of State from 1981, made little progress in the introduction of the central tenet of the free-market approach to education – a voucher scheme, while the ability of teachers to control what actually went on in schools was shown by the disruption of 1984–86. It was also noted that the competitiveness of such countries as Japan, Singapore and Taiwan was not incompatible with strong central direction in matters of education. Indeed, it was argued that higher standards of achievement in some Asian and European countries depended upon centrally prescribed and controlled curricula and assessment.

Kenneth Baker, who replaced Joseph in 1986, had no inhibitions about government action in respect of the curriculum. The idea of a national curriculum had been widely canvassed both in educational and political circles, but never achieved. Central government intervention might be justified on that ground alone, but other arguments were on hand. Central control would deprive local education authorities and teachers of yet another area of influence. Reliable national data upon the performance of individual children, schools and the system as a whole would become available for the first time. This would be of value in enabling parents, pupils and students to make informed choices about education. It would also enable the government, on behalf of the nation as a whole, to identify and deal with cases of failing teachers and schools, and to demand better value for money.

Kenneth Baker's period of office as Secretary of State for Education came to an end in 1989, and by the following year Keith Joseph's warnings about the over-prescriptive nature of the National Curriculum and the considerable burden of national testing, as originally conceived, were being echoed by members of the government. Even Margaret Thatcher, who as Prime Minster bore the ultimate responsibility for the 1988 Act, and who directly intervened in the details of the history syllabus under the National Curriculum, was beginning to doubt the wisdom of her actions.

Now the history report has come out. It is very detailed. There were not many secondary school teachers on the syllabus-forming committee . . . My worry is whether we should put out such a detailed one. You see, once you put out such an approved curriculum, if you have got it wrong, the situation is worse afterwards than it was before . . . At any given time a large number of teachers are teaching a subject extremely well. But if you take them off what they know has worked for years, far better than anyone else's syllabus, then you wonder: were you doing it right? . . . You can make it so exciting. But you cannot make it terribly exciting if a teacher is given no scope for using her creativeness. So that is really my concern.[2]

Control is exciting. The temptation to deprive others of power and to exercise it in their stead is difficult to resist. Although control and power bring both responsibility, and blame when expectations are disappointed, it is unlikely that politicians at the centre, of whatever party, will easily give up the powers that have steadily been acquired by central government since 1979.

There can be no doubt that many of the recent changes, including those which have resulted in decreased local education authority and teacher control and increased central power, have secured considerable approval among politicians of all parties and the public. For example, Tony Blair, currently leader of the Labour Party, decided to send his son to a grant-maintained school. Some schools have become grant-maintained in order to avoid the policies of Conservative-, rather than Labour-controlled local education authorities. But there has also been opposition. Free marketeers have deplored the abandonment of the voucher principle and the introduction of a centralized curriculum and testing. Critics from the Left have argued that independent schools should have been subject to more central control, for example in respect of curriculum and testing. More general criticisms regret centralized control in itself, as making education subject to political dogma and eroding true independence and diversity. Advocates of local control have argued for the superiority of locally-elected and accountable bodies over government-appointed quangos. The grant-maintained system has been seen both as divisive, and as inefficient in that competition in education is less desirable than co-operation.

HISTORICAL PERSPECTIVES

Medieval and early modern

In the medieval period both Church and state held considerable control over education. The Catholic church exercised its role through the activities of bishops and cathedral chapters, of monastic and other orders. English kings, for example Alfred in the ninth century, and Edgar in the tenth, personally encouraged the spread of education. Like the Church, the royal household and government was an employer of educated labour. Monarchs kept a jealous eye over the fortunes of the English universities, and Henry III in 1265 and Edward III in 1334 both suppressed rival foundations to Oxford and Cambridge. Kings in Parliament also legislated for the control of apprenticeship.

During the sixteenth century the relationship between Church and state was changed in a quite dramatic way. In the 1530s Henry VIII, with the approval of Parliament, made himself head of the Church. Many of the former centres of religious education, including monasteries and nunneries, were simply suppressed. In the 1540s Regius professorships, appointed by the Crown, were established at the universities. Trinity College was founded at Cambridge, and Christ Church reconstituted at Oxford. A *Royal Grammar* was prescribed for use in all grammar schools.

From this time, in spite of the restoration of Roman Catholicism in the reign of Mary Tudor in the sixteenth century, and the ascendancy of Puritanism during the period of the Interregnum in the seventeenth, the alliance between Church and state in terms of the control of education held firm. Indeed, it was to be reconstituted and strengthened with the restoration of monarchy, Anglican church and Parliament in 1660. The Act of Uniformity of 1662 required clergymen, university dons and tutors, and schoolmasters, to be Anglicans, and to be licensed by a bishop. From 1689, penalties against unlicensed teaching were relaxed, and from 1700 only masters in grammar schools were required to hold a bishop's licence.

Thus, from the 1530s until the 1830s English education was firmly controlled by the state and the state Church. The two were indissoluble, not simply as represented in the person of the monarch, but also in their identity of interest. Religious instruction in the tenets of the Established Church was not simply a preparation for a good life in this world and salvation in the next; it was also a means of ensuring political, as well as religious, orthodoxy. One of the clearest examples of this control was to be seen in the Universities of Oxford and Cambridge. From 1604 these were entitled to send members to Parliament, and Oxford, under William Laud, its reforming Chancellor and Archbishop of Canterbury, was the centre of the royalist cause in the 1640s. Oxford was to continue under royal patronage: Charles II summoned his Parliament there in 1681, and further signs of royal favour were received during the reigns of Anne and of George III. Both English universities remained under clerical control until well into the nineteenth century, and tutors were required to be both celibate and in holy orders. The purpose of the universities, as professional schools, was to educate members of the priesthood of the Anglican church. In the wider sense their aim was to ensure religious and political orthodoxy in the sons of the governing and aspiring classes.

The legislation of the 1530s also saw the formal union of England and Wales under a Tudor monarch. Wales became subject to English law in matters of education and no separate universities were established for the Principality until the nineteenth century. The union with Scotland in 1707, however, left the Scots with their separate legal system, church, and much prized system of education, which boasted more universities than those of England. Not surprisingly, English university reformers of the early nineteenth century, in seeking to provide higher education that was not controlled by Anglican clergy nor confined to the study of a medieval curriculum shaped by the needs of medieval clerics, looked to Scotland for inspiration and leadership.

One aspect of the sixteenth-century Reformation, however, promoted greater diversity of educational control within England itself. The suppression of monasteries and monastic cathedrals, chantries and religious guilds, provided a spur, and on occasion the means, for the establishment of grammar and other schools under the control of town corporations. While schools were subject to the general regulations laid down by Church and state, they also, under the terms of a variety of trust deeds, charters and statutes, were subject to the requirements of individual and group founders and benefactors.

Nineteenth century

By the beginning of the nineteenth century the control mechanisms which had survived, albeit with modification and amendment, for some 300 years, were facing a new series of changes and challenges. These stemmed from a variety of causes. The union with Ireland in 1800 and the admission of Protestant Dissenters and Roman Catholics to civil rights in the 1820s, including entry to Parliament, was a recognition that religious diversity was no longer to be equated with rebellion and treason. Population explosion, industrialization and urbanization were accompanied by a proliferation of secular knowledge and of the number and variety of forms of secular employment. The Anglican church, with its parochial organization and rural ethos, was ill suited to ministering to the needs of the new urban dwellers, some of whom became adherents of Dissenting communities, while others remained strangers both to church and chapel. The Religious Census of 1851 provided clear evidence that some 40 per cent of the population did not go to divine service on Sunday, while of those who did only the minority attended an Anglican church. In the light of these findings the claim of the Established Church to have exclusive control over the education of the nation was refuted, while even its plea for privileged status would increasingly come under threat. By the middle of the nineteenth century many promoters of education were beginning to regret the Church's control over education, and to argue that the powers of members of the episcopate in the House of Lords were being exercised to the detriment of the national interest. Though the old alliance of Church and state would not easily be broken, it was now clear that religious and political orthodoxy were no longer inextricably intertwined.

Sunday schools, the first mass educational movement of modern English society, were essentially, though not invariably under religious control. During the first half of the nineteenth century new religious organizations were established to control day schooling. Chief among these was the National Society for Promoting the Education of the Poor in the Principles of the Established Church, founded in 1811, with the Archbishop of Canterbury at its head. Other denominational bodies of the first half of the nineteenth century included the Catholic Poor School Committee and the Wesleyan Education Committee. The leading interdenominational body was the British and Foreign School Society. The original government grant of £20,000 was given to the National and British Societies for building new schools. By the 1840s the grant was being distributed more widely, although some Voluntaryists, principally Congregationalists and Baptists, refused until 1867 to accept government aid for their schools. On the eve of the Elementary Education Act of 1870, of some 8,000 state-aided elementary schools in England and Wales, some 6,000 were National schools and a further 1,500 British or Wesleyan.

After 1833 central government provided financial aid for schools ultimately under the control of religious organizations. From 1839, however, government inspection was a condition of aid. This requirement occasioned considerable controversy, so that a concordat between Church and state over the appointment and role of inspectors was hammered out in the following year. For example, all appointments of inspectors had to be approved by the societies whose schools they would visit.

The year 1839 also saw the establishment of a government department for education. The Committee of Privy Council on Education, charged to control 'the application of any sums which may be voted by Parliament for the purposes of Education in England and Wales', was originally composed of five ministers and presided over by the Lord President of the Council. Although the Committee rarely met, its first secretary, James Kay-Shuttleworth, was determined to promote state assistance to education. This aim was furthered by the management clauses of 1846 which required that schools built with government aid should include lay members on managing boards and that control of secular instruction should lie with all the managers, and not just with the clergy. Other government initiatives of 1846 included the Minutes which provided financial assistance to pupil teachers, teachers and training colleges, and a system of certification, a series of measures which gave teachers the impression that they were becoming state employees. These changes were achieved by administrative means rather than by legislation. In the 1840s, as in the 1830s, attempts to increase educational provision by statute were successfully resisted by supporters of Church and Dissent alike.

The Committee of Privy Council was an imperfect instrument, and in 1856 a vice-president of the Council was appointed to represent education in the House of Commons. At the same time the Department of Science and Art, established in 1853 under the aegis of the Board of Trade, was placed under the Committee, although it continued a separate existence at South Kensington. Expenditure and personnel grew apace, so that by 1858 the annual grant reached £836,920. The Education Department, with more than 100 employees, was one of the largest civil offices of state, and some thirty inspectors and sixteen assistants were required to oversee the grants to schools.

During the second half of the nineteenth century central government continued to develop its educational role. There was a series of commissions and reports and, subsequently, of acts. Thus there was legislation for the Universities of Oxford and Cambridge in 1854 and 1856 respectively. The report of the Clarendon Commission led to the Public Schools Act of 1868; the report of the Taunton Commission to the Endowed Schools Act of 1869. Such legislation, however, was not designed to bring secondary schools and the ancient universities under state control, simply to remove ancient anomalies and to produce a modest improvement in efficiency. Indeed, the most significant element of government educational legislation of the second half of the nineteenth century was its continuing determination to act in support of voluntary effort. Aid, moreover, was not given to the most needy, but to the most deserving.

The report of the Newcastle Commission in 1861 led not to legislation, but to the Revised Code of the following year. This Code was an administrative measure with administrative purposes – an increase in efficiency which might also lead to a reduction in government expenditure. The dangers of too great an involvement by central government in education were still widely appreciated. Moreover the report seemed to show that the voluntary system was working well. The names of nearly all children were on the school books; the problems were to ensure regular attendance, better standards, and an extension of government grants to a wider range of schools. Much of this could be achieved by more efficiency and the introduction of a little free trade – payment by results. Accordingly, a national curriculum based on the three Rs was introduced, with national testing in six standards. Central control of curriculum and assessment, therefore, was achieved, as a means of ensuring that schools could remain under voluntary control. Government ownership of schools and the direct employment of teachers was still associated in many minds with despotic and dangerous European regimes. It was both un-English and unnecessary.

Another danger foreseen by Robert Lowe, Vice-President of the Committee of Council on Education in 1862, was that

> the grant for education may become a grant to maintain the so-called vested interest of those engaged in education. If Parliament does not set a limit to this evil, such a state of things will arise that the conduct of the educational system will pass out of the hands of the Privy Council and of the House of Commons into the hands of the persons working the educational system, and then no demand they choose to make on the public purse would any Ministry dare to refuse.[3]

The Revised Code of 1862 indicated both the reluctance of central government to become more substantially involved in the provision of education itself, and a refusal to create local education authorities as recommended by the Newcastle Commissioners. Nevertheless, in the longer term the Code may be seen as symptomatic of a substantial change in control which would take place over the next hundred years. Henceforth central government grants would be given according to the proficiency of pupils in secular, as opposed to religious, knowledge.

Admirers of the education systems of France and Germany, such as Matthew Arnold and Lyon Playfair, outlined the reasons for central government to assume more, rather than less, responsibility for education, but to little avail. Initiatives came at the local level, in the 1850s in Manchester and in the 1860s in Birmingham, from groups which sought to supplement central government grants for elementary schooling with rate aid. Although, in 1868, a Conservative government, in a rare attempt to seize the educational initiative, prepared a bill to establish a Minister of Education, the Elementary Education Act of 1870 was the product of a Liberal government in which William Gladstone was Prime Minister and William Forster the Vice-President.

This measure, which established school boards in areas where there was a proven deficiency of school places after the voluntary organizations had been given a period of grace in which to provide sufficient schools, reflected Gladstone's belief that in education, as in other spheres of life, the voluntary principle was superior to that of state intervention. In introducing the bill, Forster declared that local agencies were preferable to an increase in central assistance and control. Having acknowledged the extent of the deficiency and the inability of the existing system to remedy it, he advised that

> It would be possible for the Government to attempt to supply it by defraying the expenses from the taxes; and I believe that one or two Hon. Gentlemen think it would be the best way. No doubt it would be possible for the Government to try to do this, but I believe it would be impossible for them to effect it. I believe it is not in the power of any central Department to undertake such a duty throughout the Kingdom. Consider also the enormous power it would give the central administration. Well, then, if Government cannot do it itself by central action, we must still rely upon local agency. Voluntary local agency has failed, therefore our hope is to invoke the help of municipal organization.[4]

School boards, as established under the 1870 Act, varied greatly in size and responsibility: from the fifty members of the London School Board who oversaw the schooling of more than half a million children, to rural boards with but five members and one school within their care. School boards were *ad hoc* bodies, their sole concern being elementary education. Further legislation, compulsory schooling from 1880, and free schooling from 1891, increased both their areas of responsibility and those of the voluntary bodies. These measures led to a most important change in control. In respect of schooling children were no longer, as they had been for centuries, subject ultimately to the control of their parents. Though in theory all parents could still provide for the education of their children at home rather than at school, in practice education for the children of the working classes now became synonymous with schooling. Attendance officers, many of them former policemen or soldiers, did their best to ensure that the law was obeyed. Though school boards and attendance committees might arouse considerable hostility from some parents, and pupils, for whom employment and earnings took priority over learning letters, such bodies represented an important step in the secularization and democratization of educational control. School boards, which were directly elected, provided opportunities for women and some members of the working classes to gain political experience. After some thirty years, however, they had outgrown the limited concept and framework of the 1870 Act. Some school boards promoted higher grade schools and evening classes, although it was generally understood that their powers did not extend to secondary and adult education. This was confirmed by the Cockerton Judgment of 1901, and led to the Education Act of 1902 which established the local education authorities of the twentieth century.

The terms of reference of the Bryce Commission, whose report was published in 1895, were to consider the best means of establishing a well-organized system of secondary education in England. An act of 1889 had enabled the newly formed multi-purpose local authorities to raise a penny rate for the purpose of supplying technical education, and from the following year the so-called 'Whisky money', raised from a duty on alcoholic beverages, could also be applied to this purpose. Income from these sources soon surpassed the expenditure of the Science and Art Department. As the new county councils and county boroughs gained experience in administering these grants in aid of secondary and technical education, the Conservative government, led by Balfour, decided to abolish the single-purpose school boards and to place elementary, secondary and other education, including teacher training, under the control of multi-purpose local authorities.

By the end of the nineteenth century, the administrative muddle which was the paradoxical consequence of an essentially administrative approach to educational matters by central government, had reached a crisis point. The Department of Science and Art, charged with promoting these two areas of the curriculum, had been administering grants to schools and teachers on the basis of examination performance. A budget of £56,911 in 1854 had risen to £770,430 in 1896. But, as the report of the Bryce Commission showed, this money was not being used in the most efficient way. The Department administered a series of examinations and grants which were neither well related to the needs of the schools, nor co-ordinated with the policies of the Education Department at Whitehall.

One outcome of the Bryce Report was an act of 1899 which established a Board of Education which subsumed the work of the Education Department, the Science and Art Department and the educational work of the Charity Commissioners. The Board, consisting of a Lord President and other ministers, became a fiction, and never met. Nevertheless, in administrative terms it represented an advance upon the previous situation. It also reflected a considerable change from the beginning of the century, when the idea of a government department, independent of the Church, to superintend and co-ordinate the nation's education would have seemed impossible. Yet the Board and its president, in contrast with the situations in some other countries in which ministers of education were making policy, providing schools and employing teachers as part of the development of the modern national state, also showed the relative paucity of central control. The Board of Education was merely charged with 'the superintendence of matters relating to education in England and Wales'. In the twentieth century, as in the nineteenth, whilst the continued use of regulations and codes enabled central government to prescribe in detailed fashion many aspects of such matters as curriculum and examinations, it did not encourage the promotion of overall policy.

Three broad political positions in respect of control of education in England had emerged by the end of the nineteenth century. Radical politicians were identified with free, compulsory, unsectarian (even secular) schooling. Some were highly suspicious of the control a corrupt central government might exercise over education, but as the century wore on the necessity for considerable state intervention and control, even for a state-provided system of education, became more widely accepted. The existence of so many private and voluntary schools, coupled with the huge expense which a state takeover of schools would entail, and the failure of Radicals to form a government, rendered such a solution improbable.

Tories, and their Conservative successors from the 1830s, on the other hand, were closely identified with the Anglican church. Their initial opposition to central government intervention in education diminished when, from the 1840s, it became clear that the system of grants in aid to voluntary bodies would greatly benefit the schools and training colleges of the Established Church. Although the 1870 Act allowed the voluntary bodies a period of grace in which to fill up the gaps in school provision, the gaps were so large that school boards, some 2,500 of them by the end of the century, were soon dotted across the land. School boards not only had access to government grants, but also to local rates. Private working-class schools were squeezed out, and by 1900 many voluntary schools, which were relying only on central government grants and voluntary subscriptions, were facing the same threat.

The main framework of English education in the nineteenth century was created by Whig and Liberal governments. It was a system of caution and compromise – steering a middle course between those Radicals who wanted a full-blown state system, and those Conservatives who wished to leave matters largely in the hands of private individuals and voluntary bodies. The Liberal compromise of 1870, recognizing the weaknesses of voluntaryism but unwilling to contemplate the responsibilities, extension of power, and increased expenditure which government schools would require, opted instead for a local solution as a further prop to the voluntary system.

Twentieth century

The Education Act of 1902, which laid the basis of the control mechanisms of the twentieth century, was the first piece of educational legislation to make provisions across the various divides of the Victorian system. It appeared, moreover, to produce for the Conservatives that most satisfying of situations – an identification of national and party interests. The school boards, with their connotations of radicalism and extravagance, were abolished, and replaced by 318 local education authorities comprising sixty-three county councils, eighty-two county boroughs, and 173 non-county boroughs and urban districts (the Part III authorities) which had power over elementary education only. In contrast the county councils and county boroughs were charged not only to provide elementary education but also to 'take such steps as seem to them desirable, to supply or aid the supply of education other than elementary education, and to promote the general co-ordination of all forms of education'. Secondary schools, teacher training colleges and adult education centres now developed under local control. Further assistance was given to the voluntary schools, which in 1902 were still more than twice as numerous as the board schools, and educating more than three million children, as opposed to the two and a half million of the board schools. While the provision and repair of school buildings remained with the voluntary bodies, other costs, including the payment of teachers' salaries, were to be met from public funds.

Although many school board personnel continued into the employment of the new local education authorities, the new Directors of Education or Chief Education Officers (CEOs) became considerably more powerful and influential than the school board clerks. CEOs were not simply administrators who serviced committees. They were educational professionals who not only became adept at resisting the interventions of the Board of Education, but who also shaped the educational systems in their own areas in accordance with their personal priorities and philosophies. Notable CEOs included James Graham of Leeds, Spurley Hey of Manchester and Percival Sharp of Sheffield (jointly known as 'the Three Musketeers' for their somewhat cavalier treatment of the Board of Education), Robert Blair of the London County Council, Henry Morris of Cambridgeshire, and the longest serving of all, William Brockington, who guided the fortunes of education in Leicestershire from 1903 until 1947.

Such local independence, which continued after the 1944 Act, may be interpreted in two ways. By 1974 education in England was still largely in the hands of some 100 local education authorities which provided the schools and employed the teachers (albeit with the majority of money coming from central government funds), but which differed widely in size and population, in the ways in which the schools systems were organized, and in the amount of money spent per pupil. Some observers continued to see such diversity as an admirable manifestation of local democracy, able to recognize and respond swiftly to changes in local circumstances and priorities. Others viewed local control as over-politicized and inefficient, a patchwork of petty tyrannies which had frustrated the development of a new concept of national education in the twentieth century.

One clearly recognizable feature of the twentieth century, however, was the steady decline in church control over schools. From 1870 the British and Foreign Society's interest in school provision rapidly waned, and many of its establishments were simply handed over to the school boards. Provision and maintenance of school buildings proved to be a considerable burden for voluntary bodies after 1902, and in 1944 many Church of England schools accepted 'controlled' status, whereby schools were financed and managed as if they were council schools, although the church authorities retained ownership in principle and could appoint one-third of the managers. Under the 1944 Act, however, Roman Catholic, and some other church schools, opted for 'voluntary aided' status, whereby building and repair grants of up to 50 per cent were provided from public funds, a percentage subsequently substantially increased. In these ways the control of the majority of English schools passed from religious into secular hands.

In the first decade of the twentieth century, as local education authorities began to establish their secondary schools, Robert Morant, secretary to the Board of Education, extended the principle of central control by means of grants and curriculum prescription, into the secondary field. This enabled the Board to insist upon the provision of a percentage of free or scholarship places within aided secondary schools. The regulations of 1904 not only laid down the subjects to be studied, but also the minimum numbers of hours to be allotted to each. This second requirement was removed some three years later, while the relaxation of curriculum control in elementary schools was signalled by the title of the *Handbook of Suggestions for the Consideration of Teachers and others concerned in the work of Public Elementary Schools*, first issued in 1905. The work of the Education Department was rationalized, with separate branches established for elementary, secondary and technical areas. A medical branch was created in 1907, and a universities branch in 1910. Although educational provision was directly under local control, central government continued to provide at least 50 per cent of the funds. This arrangement often led to difficulties – as for example in the sorry story of continuation schooling as laid down under the Education Act of 1918, an episode that was repeated with the county colleges envisaged under the 1944 Act. In such instances central government might determine policies, even enshrine them in legislation, but the implementation of such policies depended upon the united commitment of both central and local authorities and their injection of substantial new funds.

In 1911 a report on examinations in secondary schools by the Board of Education's Consultative Committee marked the growing interest of central government in this field. In 1917 a Secondary School Examinations Council was established with representatives from universities, teachers and local authorities, under a chairman appointed by the Board, to advise the Board on rationalization of examinations. This led to the nationally recognized School Certificate and subsequent General Certificate of Education (GCE) examinations. In the twentieth century, as in the nineteenth, the universities played a leading role in controlling school-leaving examinations. The 1960s saw the introduction of the Certificate of Secondary Education (CSE) examination, and by the 1990s the GCE Ordinary level and CSE examinations had given way to the General Certificate of Secondary Education (GCSE) examination. These examinations were the product, ultimately, of central government decisions, but their content and conduct was in the hands of examining bodies which were not under direct government control.

Both the 1918 and the 1944 Acts continued, indeed expanded, the roles of the local education authorities, although in both cases it appeared, at first, that central government was going to assume greater control and direction over the system as a whole. Under the 1918 Act compulsory school attendance to age 14 was secured, the age subsequently being raised to 15 in 1947 and 16 in 1972. The 1944 Act finally established a Ministry of Education, headed by a Minister whose duty it would be 'to promote the education of the people of England and Wales . . . and to secure the effective execution by local authorities, under his control and direction, of the national policy of providing a varied and comprehensive educational service in every area'. At first sight it appeared that with the Minister (as opposed to the President) education would come more closely under central control. The redesignation of education as being organized in 'a continuous process conducted in three successive stages' of primary, secondary and further, betokened a greater uniformity of provision and practice, but the stuttering progress of secondary school comprehensive reorganization, whereby four years after the issue of Circular 10/65 which requested local education authorities to submit plans within twelve months, eighteen authorities had still not done so, indicated the limitations of central control in practice. Some thirty years later, grammar schools still exist in some local education authorities.

During the 1960s, when expansion was the major educational theme, issues of control seemed to be of less importance. After 1973, however, economic crises, unemployment and declining school rolls led to more central intervention in the search for accountability, efficiency and measurable improvement of standards. This was the message of James Callaghan's Ruskin College speech of 1976; it was reformulated and reiterated in Conservative educational policies from 1979.

One theme to emerge in the 1970s, a theme which bestrode Labour and Conservative administrations, was that of increasing the powers of governing bodies. During the nineteenth century managers of elementary schools and governors of secondary schools had exercised considerable authority. Although, under the 1944 Act, it was intended that each primary school should have a managing body, and each secondary school a governing body, with responsibility for the general direction of the conduct and curriculum of the school, in some areas schools were grouped together for these purposes, while in others effective control lay in the hands of the local education authority or the head teacher. The Taylor Report of 1977 concluded that in many areas of England control exercised by managing and governing bodies was seriously deficient. It recommended a governing body for each school, with real powers, and with representation from four groups: local education authority, teachers, parents, local community. The 1980 Act began the process of implementing these recommendations, a process confirmed by the Education (No. 2) Act of 1986 and the Education Reform Act of 1988.

The Education Reform Act substantially increased the control of central government over school curricula and testing, abolished the ILEA, and weakened the power of other local education authorities by the removal of polytechnics and colleges from their control, the local management of schools, and the facility for schools to opt out of local education authority control altogether and to become grant-maintained. In 1996 it is apparent that since 1979, and particularly since 1988, local education authorities have been reduced from their former pivotal role in the education system. In some parts of the country, indeed, they may come to occupy virtually a residual position. That residue may consist in providing a limited range of services which grant-maintained schools cannot supply on an individual basis, or in catering for those schools, and pupils, which do not flourish in a market system.

In contrast, central government control has increased, though such control may depend ultimately upon finance, and is infrequently exercised directly by the central Department but rather through such bodies as the Further Education Funding Council and the Teacher Training Agency.

CONCLUSION

Six conclusions may be drawn from the historical perspective.

The first is the complexity of the issues. Control is both formal and informal. It depends not only upon statute and regulation, but also upon individuals and ideologies. In some instances control may be exercised to produce specific educational goals, in others to ensure that the actual process of education is as efficient (and cheap) as possible, though the ends may not be specified. Political, administrative and ideological issues may become intertwined. For example, a government may introduce educational reform under the guise or the reality of improved administrative efficiency, but for the broad purpose of promoting a particular ideology which is linked to its own political prospects. Education, moreover, is so vast, so all-pervasive, that it must, necessarily, be subject to different controllers – parents, teachers, administrators, clerics, politicians, etc. – and to competing ideologies: private and public, secular and religious, professional and liberal. The realities of control are not easily identifiable. At times in history those who have been technically in control of certain situations have allowed their powers to be exercised by others, either by choice or through default. Although it is dangerous to generalize, this last feature seems to have been particularly characteristic of education in England, as opposed to the situation in some other countries. Indeed, in contrast with many systems overseas, education in England often seems to have been either out of control or controlled by somewhat invisible forces, including those of tradition and social class.

The second conclusion is that the three elements of control – persons, means and purposes – have undergone substantial change in the twentieth century. The radical reforms that have taken place since 1979 must be set against an even more fundamental change that has occurred in the last hundred years – the rise of the secular society. For much of English history the Church (Catholic in the middle ages, and Anglican from the Reformation) had considerable control over education, supplied the means of formal schooling through teachers, study materials and premises, and did so for the purpose of promoting the good life both in this world and in the next. By the later nineteenth century that situation was rapidly changing. Christian ideology and culture was being challenged, and steadily supplanted. Though it would be wrong to minimize the influence of Christian and other faiths in contemporary England, and though the residual commitment of central government to religious purposes in education was shown in the Education Reform Act of 1988 (in imitation of the legislation of 1944), in the 1990s it is central government that exercises control over education, its means are schools and teachers subject to a competitive culture, and its purposes are to promote individual and national affluence while expending as small an amount as possible.

A third perspective relates recent Conservative reforms, and particularly the Education Reform Act of 1988, to the legislation of 1870, 1902 and 1944. Though school boards from 1870, and local education authorities from 1902, have played a substantial role in controlling education in England, it is important to notice that prior to 1870 there were no such bodies. The establishment of a central government body for English education in 1839 preceded the introduction of local government agencies by some thirty years. Conservative policies since 1979, therefore, may be seen essentially as reverting to a pre-1870 situation. In 1902 the Conservative government of Arthur Balfour put paid to the London School Board on account of its *ad hoc* nature, its high levels of expenditure, and its tendency to engage in activities outside its designated sphere. In 1988 the Conservative government of Margaret Thatcher brought the Inner London Education Authority to an end on the very same grounds. It might be argued that, in terms of central government control, the one was a logical development of the other.

An even closer match may be found in terms of curriculum. The National Curriculum established under the 1988 Act was firmly based on the secondary school regulations of 1904, which followed the 1902 Act. In 1902 one Conservative government, on the grounds of promoting national efficiency, replaced one type of local education authority by another. In 1988 another Conservative government decided that national efficiency required the emasculation, even abolition of all local education authorities and a return to the former situation of individual and professional effort, aided by central government.

As for the relationship between the Acts of 1944 and 1988, it can be suggested that, in terms of control, once again the one was a logical development of the other. During the debates on the 1944 bill the *Times Educational Supplement* urged that 'forty years of lack of effective power at the centre have amply proved the absolute necessity for central direction and control'.[5] Although, under the terms of that Act, the President of the Board was replaced by a Minister of Education, during the next forty years the same comment might well have been made. Those who framed the 1944 Act did not have a clear concept of the role of the central authority in education, nor of its relationship with the other partners in the education service.

A fourth issue, which also results in part from the decision taken in 1870, concerns the means of control. In the nineteenth century, governments found it possible to control elementary schools through a combination of apportioning grants, and the direction of teacher training, school curricula and examinations. In England, central government neither owned schools nor employed teachers. The ideological shift that took place in many other countries, whereby central (or local) government assumed the ownership of and the responsibility for the educational system, did not occur in England. When, in the 1860s, teachers began to imagine that they were indeed becoming employees of central government, with a right to patronage and protection, Robert Lowe swiftly disabused them of such pretensions. By the end of the century religious control of education was declining, but the central government did not step in to fill the breach.

In the twentieth century teacher training was transmuted into teacher education, and came more under the control of universities and colleges. The control of school curricula became a very hazy area indeed, in practice lying somewhere between local education authorities, governors, head teachers, teachers and examination boards.

In 1979 a Conservative government came into power with the belief that Robert Lowe's fears about the rise of the education estate had been fulfilled, that its local administrators and teachers had outgrown their controllers, and created a state within a state with its own priorities and values. Two alternatives were available. The first was for central government to take over the direct ownership of schools and the employment of teachers (a most unlikely occurrence given the Conservative policies of advancing private, as opposed to public, ownership). The second was to exercise control in the 1980s and 1990s as it had been in the 1880s and 1890s, in such areas as teacher education, school curricula and examinations. This process involved diminishing the control exercised in these areas by higher education institutions, teacher controlled bodies such as the Schools Council, teachers themselves, and local education authorities. The path, however, was not an easy one. Indeed, one feature of the reassumption of control of the education system by central government was the demonstration of how ill-prepared, in terms of personnel and expertise, central government was to exercise control by these relatively restricted means.

Another conclusion to be drawn is in respect of partnership. The doctrine of control through partnership in education is a noble one. In 1944 R. A. Butler, in conscious reversal of Robert Lowe's comment on public education during the passage of the Education Bill of 1870 that 'instead of leading boldly, we follow timidly', stated 'that the Central Authority shall lead boldly and not follow timidly'. Nevertheless, he also immediately added the qualification that 'in no sense shall we take away the spirit of partnership which we desire from the local authorities'.[6] Whether the years following the Second World War should be seen as a classic era of partnership is debatable. On the one hand the concept of partnership was frequently mentioned, and no single group – central government, local authorities, churches, employers, teachers, parents, students – exercised unfettered control over the system. On the other hand it could be argued that partnership was a matter of rhetoric rather than of reality, and that the separate groups went their separate ways, defending their own interests with little perception of, or concern for, the greater good.

The supposed partnership of the years since 1945 was not well developed. There were considerable gaps, for example between teacher educators and classroom teachers, and between teachers and parents. Divisions between teacher unions hampered their chances of developing the real professional control, which was presumed to exist, of what went on in the classroom, and so frequently envied by those teachers in other countries who felt borne down by central direction of their employment and careers, and by centrally prescribed curricula and textbooks. When, from 1979, and particularly from 1987, the era of partnership was replaced by an era of confrontation, the other partners in the educational process did not unite against central government in any effective way. Perhaps effective resistance was impossible, as the parental ballot of over 90 per cent in favour of the retention of the ILEA showed, but there is a sense in which in England, as opposed to Scotland, divide and rule was an easy option.

One reason for the failure to develop a coherent partnership was the nature of change in the period between 1944 and 1972. For this was an era of expansion, in which all those involved in the process of education could participate with benefit. When, from the mid-1970s, it became apparent that future educational reforms would require greater production for less investment, scapegoats for the unsatisfactory elements of English education would need to be found. Confrontation replaced partnership. So far the losers in that confrontation have been local education authorities, teacher educators and teachers. When, as in 1995, it became apparent that the losers might also include pupils and students, new alliances and partnerships were formed – for example of parents, governors, teachers, local education authorities, and even employers – against a central government that was perceived to be creating problems by a policy of under-funding, but seeking to devolve the blame for such problems to the periphery.

Finally, it should be noted that many schools and other educational activities have always been subject to private and individual control. This was true of a considerable number of schools in the nineteenth century, while even those that were nominally claimed for the National and other voluntary school societies, frequently enjoyed quite tenuous relationships with such bodies. The historical record shows that in modern times central government intervention in educational matters has been prompted largely by a concern for the efficient use of public funds. Vision has been sorely lacking, and in consequence central governments in England, both those of the nineteenth century and of the twentieth, have failed to generate a shared ethos of excellence through national education. This relationship between funding, quality and control was demonstrated most clearly when independent schools were excluded from the curricular and assessment provisions of the Education Reform Act of 1988; their independence and quality being taken as a matter of fact. In the 1960s and 1970s Labour governments were highly circumspect (or dilatory) in exercising control over those elements of the education scene that might have been presumed to be inimical to the general ideology and specific political and administrative interests which the party espoused. The control of education by Conservative governments since 1979 to promote general ideology, party political (and arguably national) interests through radical legislation from the Right, may well prompt a future government of the Left not only to reverse part of that agenda, but also to promote a quite different policy, not least in respect of independent schools.

NOTES

1. Lester Smith, 1945, 15.
2. *Sunday Telegraph*, 1 April 1990.
3. Quoted in Maclure, 1970, 6.
4. Quoted in Maclure, 1969, 101–2.
5. *Times Educational Supplement*, 12 February 1944
6. Quoted in Aldrich and Leighton, 1985, 22.

SUGGESTED READING

Aldrich, R. and Leighton, P. (1985) *Education: Time for a New Act?*
Bishop, A. (1971) *The Rise of a Central Authority for English Education.*
Gosden, P. H. J. H. (1966) *The Development of Educational Administration in England and Wales.*
Regan, D. (1979) *Local Government and Education.*
Murphy, J. (1970) *Church, State and Schools in Britain, 1800–1970.*
Sharp, P. and Dunford, J. (1990) *The Education System in England and Wales.*
Tomlinson, J. (1993) *The Control of Education.*
Vaizey, J. (1963) *The Control of Education.*

SIX
Economic Performance

CURRENT ISSUES

By the broadest international standards England (and the United Kingdom) has a sound economy, with high levels of production and a good standard of living. Visitors to this country from those of the Third World and former Communist states may, with reason, marvel at the high percentages of ownership of homes and of consumer durables, at the range and quality of goods in the shops, at the facilities for public and private transport. But historical and other contemporary comparisons and contrasts provide a different perspective. For much of the nineteenth century Britain was the world's leading industrial power. Even in 1950 British people enjoyed one of the highest standards of living in the world. Although, after 1945, the economy grew on average by some 2.4 per cent per year, and the standard of living overall by some 2 per cent per year, growth in some other countries was much greater.

Why did this happen? British economic growth had not slowed since the nineteenth century; rather the reverse. Though some caution must be urged in respect of comparability of figures over long periods of time, the general trends are clear. The growth in the economy of some 2.4 per cent since the Second World War may be contrasted with a growth of only 0.9 per cent between 1913 and 1950, 1.0 per cent between 1870 and 1913, and 1.5 per cent between 1820 and 1870, the heyday of the industrial revolution.[1] After 1945 the opening up of world markets and of world trade, and the rapid application of scientific and technological inventions (many of them British) to manufacturing production, provided the opportunities for substantial economic growth. The relative failure of British products and producers, however, either to apply these inventions or to compete successfully in such markets, soon became apparent. This was particularly evident in respect of manufactures. Between 1979 and 1989, two boom years, manufacturing output in the United Kingdom rose by 13 per cent. Over the same period West German output rose three times as quickly; that of Japan five times.[2] For example, from a base of 100 in 1975, by 1990 industrial production in the United Kingdom had barely reached 110. In sharp contrast, that of the USA was in excess of 130, of West Germany nearly 180, while Japanese industrial production had grown to a staggering

260.[3] In 1993 manufacturing output in the United Kingdom was no higher than it had been twenty years previously, while that of West Germany had doubled.[4]

One effect of this stagnation in industrial output, accompanied as it was by automation, computerization and the elimination of many inefficient work practices, was a considerable reduction in the size of the industrial workforce. In 1979, when Margaret Thatcher first came to power, some eight million people were employed in manufacturing; fifteen years later that figure had been almost halved.[5] Clear evidence of the overall increase in wealth and of the relative decline of British manufacturing in the face of foreign competition was to be found in the numbers and origins of the cars and motor cycles which throng our streets, and of the televisions, washing machines and hi-fi equipment which inhabit our homes.

Of course industrial output is not the only means of wealth creation, nor of employment. For example the economies of some countries are built upon extractive industries, and in recent years North Sea oil has become a vital lubricant of the British economy. Another dimension, recently emphasised by Rubinstein both in contemporary and historical terms, is that 'Britain's economy was *always, even during the period 1815–70*, primarily a commercial/financial-oriented economy'.[6] To some extent the decline in industrial employment was compensated by a considerable increase in employment in the service sector. For example, between 1984 and 1988 jobs in banking, finance and insurance grew from 1.6 million to 2.5 million; in hotels and catering from 995,000 to 1.6 million.[7] In 1987, amongst the twelve members of the European Community, the United Kingdom, though last in the percentage of its population employed in agriculture, and only seventh in terms of industrial occupations, still ranked third (behind Belgium and the Netherlands) in the percentage of its people employed in services.[8] In 1993 the United Kingdom had the highest percentage of the population aged 16 or over that was economically active (in work or seeking work) of any country in the Community, except Denmark.[9]

Nevertheless, despite the caveats, there is sufficient evidence about the relative decline of the British economy, coupled with other factors such as a marked increase in the inequitable distribution of wealth within the country, to produce considerable concern. Though wealth creation and a rising standard of living are not the only, perhaps even the most important, goals in the existence of an individual or of a nation, such goals are both quantifiable and widely shared, and also facilitate the provision of basic services – hospitals, schools, libraries, etc. – which command even broader approval. Of course all countries are concerned about the state of their own economies, but an issue of even greater concern must be the fact that of the five billion inhabitants of this planet the richest fifth enjoy some 58 per cent of the world's wealth; the poorest fifth a mere 4 per cent.[10]

Economic performance is related to education in at least two ways: those of consumption and of investment. In the first instance, as indicated above, the state of the economy influences the amount of resources that can be made available to support education. For example, a poor country, with low levels of literacy may, as the result of the discovery and exploitation of some natural resource such as oil, be able to provide a system of universal schooling, with impressive levels of buildings and equipment, and well-qualified and highly paid teachers. That is not to say, however, that the wealthiest countries necessarily invest most in their educational systems. Nor would it appear to be true that the largest financial investments in education always produce the best educational results.

If the relationships between national wealth and investment in education, and between investment in education and educational outcomes, are problematic, that between investment in education and economic outcomes is even more difficult to determine. One starting point which seems to confirm the value, at least at a personal level, of investment in education for the purpose of economic gain, relates to the income levels and employability of individuals. Several studies, both in the United Kingdom and in other countries, have indicated that, in general, the higher the level of academic qualification the higher the income: for example those with higher degrees or equivalent on average earn more than those with first degrees or equivalent, who in turn earn more than those with a school-leaving qualification at 18, and so on.[11] Similarly, a Labour Force Survey of 1987 showed that the unemployment rate in the United Kingdom of young people with higher education qualifications was some 4 per cent, as opposed to more than 8 per cent of well-qualified 18-year-old school leavers, and over 15 per cent for those with few or no educational qualifications.[12] Such evidence, of course, does not necessarily mean that more wealth is being created, but rather that those with higher educational qualifications are acquiring a larger percentage of such wealth as does exist. Nor is it always true that the ablest members of society invariably achieve the highest educational qualifications. A variety of other factors – wealth, social class, gender, ethnic group – influence the ability of individuals to succeed within the formal educational system.

The positive nature of the relationship between educational attainment on the one hand and economic earnings and employability on the other, when extended to international comparisons, may be seen as a way of laying the relative decline in British economic performance at the door of education. Comparative studies of educational achievement are always problematic, but there is a considerable amount of evidence that within the United Kingdom general educational standards (as opposed to those of the highest achievers) are low. This was confirmed by a recent survey which measured the educational attainments of British youngsters against those of three of her major economic competitors, and concluded that

> overall standards of attainment amongst 16–18 year olds in the UK are significantly lower than in Germany, France and Japan, and indeed, than in a number of other major countries. Whilst the top 5% of attainers do as well as in any other country, a considerably lower proportion of the rest achieve general standards in core areas of general education or in vocational skills, and this despite a steady rate of improvement in qualification levels. As a consequence the workforce in the UK is under-qualified by comparison with competitor countries, with less than 30% holding intermediate level vocational qualifications compared with West Germany's 60%.[13]

Though Steedman and Green emphasised shortcomings in the education of the majority, as opposed to the minority, of British pupils, in the context of employment, a similar situation is to be found at boardroom level. Few of the United Kingdom's top managers (less than 30 per cent) are university graduates, as opposed to 85 per cent in Japan and the USA, and 62 per cent in France and West Germany.[14] This situation, in which poorly qualified managers continue to recruit poorly qualified staff, without any great perception of the need to improve either their own qualifications or those of their employees, has been tellingly defined by David Finegold as a 'low skill equilibrium'.[15]

The dangers of such an equilibrium are apparent in a static situation; they are likely to be compounded if future economic success depends essentially upon a considerable increase in the possession and application of knowledge. According to a report from the University of Warwick, between 1970 and 1990 the number of jobs in the UK grew by some 1.8 million, to just under 26 million. Over the same period, however, the pattern of employment changed considerably. More than one million skilled manual jobs disappeared, as did 1.8 million for less skilled manual workers. In contrast, more than three million managerial, professional and technical jobs were created. The same study predicted that by the year 2000 there would be 10.5 million managerial, professional and technical jobs, as opposed to 7.3 million skilled, and less skilled, manual jobs. This would represent a complete reversal of the traditional situation which obtained until quite recently whereby manual jobs were more numerous.[16] Prediction of future employment trends is a difficult business. Though there may be fewer skilled and unskilled manual workers in industrial employment, other opportunities, for example in construction work, may develop.

Though the Report of the National Commission drew attention to the loss of manual jobs, an area which would appear to be at greater risk is that of clerical employment, even in such areas as banking and other financial services. An even more fundamental issue which may connect the worlds of education and economic performance is that of unemployment. Few now believe either in the possibility of full employment or in the capacity of governments or the market to ensure that jobs can be shared between those who wish to work. Indeed, the obverse appears to be true: that successful economies will depend upon the employment of the ablest and best qualified for as long as possible, to the exclusion of their less capable contemporaries.

In concluding this section three broad issues in respect of the relationship between education and economic performance in England may be identified. The first is the amount of public investment in education. This appears to be consistent with investment levels in competitor countries, superior indeed to those of Germany and Japan, although the greater strength of such economies may mean that their actual amounts expended per pupil are higher. Such broad comparability naturally raises questions about the nature and effectiveness of the investment. On the one hand it could be argued that it is sufficient to invest in human beings, in human capital, in as general and open a manner as possible. The alternative view, which has predominated since the later 1970s, is that public investment in education should be targeted towards specific economic and social ends.

This latter approach raises issues of control, curriculum and standards. Is education to improve economic performance to be directed by central or local government, or by the choices of pupils and students? Should school curricula concentrate on basic literacy and numeracy, place science and technology at the core, concentrate upon specific vocational skills, or be infused by an entrepreneurial ethos throughout? Is some combination of these purposes possible? Is the key simply to raise standards across the board, so that British workers, at every level, are more knowledgeable, more skilled, more entrepreneurial, more conscientious, more healthy than their competitors in other countries?

The third issue concerns education in its widest sense, and the relationship between school and society. Given the high educational achievements of the minority in the English educational system, and the low levels of attainment and of post-compulsory participation of the majority, the very function of schooling in English society must be called into question. It would appear that schools and the examination systems have been used as a filtering mechanism for entry to higher education and to the professions, rather than concentrating upon providing a skilled, motivated, entrepreneurial culture for all.

HISTORICAL PERSPECTIVES

Medieval education was essentially vocational, and schooling a means of preparing for a particular set of clerical occupations. Much education took place in the family where girls learned about their future roles in life from their mothers, and boys from their fathers. Land was the main source of wealth and most occupations were rural, or rurally based. More formal vocational training might take place in the household of a noble or master, or through apprenticeship. During the sixteenth and seventeenth centuries commercial and industrial enterprises grew in importance. By the later eighteenth century Britain was poised to lead the first industrial revolution of modern times.

Industrial revolutions

England's transformation from an agriculturally based nation to one whose main sources of wealth and employment were to be found in commerce and industry took place in the late eighteenth and nineteenth centuries. This transformation was reflected in population explosion, urbanization, and changes in employment. The census first took place in 1801 and, apart from 1941, has been held every ten years since that date. Between 1801 and 1911 the population of England grew at more than 10 per cent in each decade, so that numbers doubled by 1851 and doubled again by 1911. The most rapid increases occurred in the booming industrial and commercial centres. In 1901 the population of Bradford was 13,000, that of Southampton, 8,000. By 1911 these had reached 288,000 and 119,000 respectively, by which date three-quarters of the population lived in towns. Reliable census data on occupations in Britain exists from 1841. In that year some 1,434,000 males were employed in agriculture, horticulture and forestry. Ten years later the figure had risen to 1,788,000, but thereafter, in spite of the overall rise in population, declined steadily, to 1,339,000 by 1901. In sharp contrast, over the same period, 1841 to 1901, the numbers of males employed in metal manufacture and associated trades grew from 396,000 to 1,485,000, in mines and quarries from 218,000 to 931,000, and in transport and communications from 196,000 to 1,409,000. Female employees in textiles and clothing trebled from 558,000 to 1,695,000. In spite of the great incidence of poverty in nineteenth-century Britain, and though there has been considerable debate over the nature and extent of the distribution of wealth, there can be little doubt that the first industrial revolution produced an overall rise in the standard of living which continued into the twentieth century.[17]

British successes in the first industrial revolution were generally acknowledged and triumphally displayed at the Great Exhibition held in the Crystal Palace in London in 1851. The causes of these successes are more difficult to identify. Much depends upon the actual nature of that phenomenon generally referred to as the 'first industrial revolution'. Should it be interpreted as a single revolution, or rather was it a series of connected but essentially discrete changes? Was it indeed primarily industrial, or rather commercial? General predisposing factors appear to have included the ready availability of natural resources – coal, iron and water – and a near monopoly in the production of cotton goods, even though all raw materials had to be imported and many of the finished products were subsequently exported. Population explosion at home ensured an abundant supply of labour and a home market, while a revolution in transport, which depended in large part upon the application of steam power, facilitated the distribution of raw materials and goods both at home and abroad. Changes were spearheaded by an expanding middle class, many of whom as Dissenters were virtually excluded from positions in public life and the professions. Notwithstanding riots and other expressions of discontent which occurred during and immediately after the French Revolutionary and Napoleonic Wars, throughout the nineteenth century Britain enjoyed relative constitutional and political stability, and experienced neither domestic revolution nor (apart from the Crimean War of 1854–56) major foreign conflict.

Two further factors merit attention: the first, technical ingenuity; the second, the application of such ingenuity to industrial and commercial ends, and the development of a mass market. The late eighteenth and early nineteenth centuries not only produced a great galaxy of engineers and inventors – Richard Arkwright, James Brindley, Samuel Crompton, James Hargreaves, James Watt – they also witnessed the successful application of their ideas for the purposes of wealth creation. In no area was this more apparent than in the manufacture of cotton goods. Between 1780 and 1860 the application of technical ingenuity reduced the cost of cloth production by 2.5 per cent per year, so that by 1860 it was possible to produce cloth at one-eighth of the cost of 1780. A piece of cloth that sold for some 70 or 80 shillings in the 1780s would cost a mere five shillings by the 1850s.[18]

To what extent can British success in the first industrial revolution be attributed to educational factors? It would appear that by the late eighteenth century basic literacy had reached the 40 per cent level which has been seen as necessary for sustained industrial take off. But, during the classic period of the first industrial revolution, literacy rates fell in many of the boom towns, as some of the least educated were sucked in to provide factory fodder, and rapid population growth outstripped the provision of schools and churches. There was no national system of education in the country as a whole. The English universities were in a relatively moribund state and certainly not at the forefront of technological advance. The late eighteenth century and early nineteenth have been characterized as the period of the 'Scottish Enlightenment' and some direct connections can be made between technological advances and the Universities of Edinburgh and Glasgow. Many Scotsmen were to the fore in the industrial revolution and some, like George Birkbeck, assumed the duty of supplying technical and vocational education to working men. But it would be difficult to argue that the first industrial revolution was the product of a national system of vocational education, although the work of the Science and Art Department, established in 1853 as a result of the Great Exhibition, did provide some means for the encouragement of more systematic technical and vocational education thereafter.

Although concerns about the quality of British workmanship and technical skills were expressed in the 1830s, and led to government intervention in the shape of schools of art, Peter Mathias has argued that Britain had achieved a technical supremacy in Europe, and that one of the most important dimensions of such superiority was that technical advance took place in an industrial and entrepreneurial, rather than in a governmental, systematic or academic context. One technical breakthrough led to another: in cotton production the flying shuttle led inexorably to the spinning jenny. Men such as Brindley and Hargreaves were illiterate, but they were members of a pioneering if motley band, characterized by Mathias as

> inspired amateurs, or brilliant artisans, trained as clock-makers, millwrights, blacksmiths or in the Birmingham trades . . . mainly local men, empirically trained, with local horizons, often very interested in things scientific, aware men, responding directly to a particular problem.[19]

Other commentators, for example Barnett, have placed less emphasis upon British technical achievement, and more upon 'a happy set of historical and geographical coincidences', notably the existence of 'abundant water power, coal and iron conveniently adjacent to each other'.[20]

During the second half of the nineteenth century that happy set of historical and geographical coincidences was put to the test. The poor performance of British exhibitors at the Paris Exhibition of 1867 sounded a warning note, and other countries, notably Germany and the United States, were to the fore in the second industrial revolution, a revolution which took place between 1870 and 1914, and was based upon precision engineering, electronics, mass production and chemical products. British shortcomings in these areas became particularly apparent during the First World War, when British technology was shown to be deficient in the manufacture of machine tools, ball bearings, magnetos, internal combustion engines and scientific and optical instruments. Even the established industries of iron and steel were technically backward, and Barnett argued that Britain 'was well on the way to becoming a technological colony of the United States and Germany'.[21]

Not all analyses of Britain's position at the end of the nineteenth century are so critical. Naturally, given the rise of major competitors, Britain's monopoly position was lost, while the vast resources and rapid population growth of the United States indicated her emergence as the world's leading industrial power. But in some areas British supremacy continued, for example in 1913 her coal output and consumption of raw cotton were both greater than those of Germany, while the tonnage of British merchant shipping exceeded that of Germany and the USA combined.[22]

Explanations of British failure in the second industrial revolution are as legion as those for her success in the first: an understandable reluctance to invest in new machinery and work practices, given that existing plant was still profitable; an abundant supply of cheap labour; the protected markets of the Empire. These factors not only accounted for the failure to modernize existing industries, but also inhibited the development of new ones. It is also apparent that the skills and techniques that were applicable to the first industrial revolution were less appropriate to the second. The technical developments which characterized the second revolution did result from the formal application of applied science, and therefore did require formal technical training and education.

The connection between foreign industrial competition and education was apparent to many in Britain, not least to the Liberal MP, ironmaster and engineer, Bernhard Samuelson, who in 1867 produced a comparative study of European technical education. In 1882 he was appointed chairman of a Royal Commission charged

> To inquire into the instruction of the industrial classes of certain foreign countries in technical and other subjects for the purpose of comparison with that of the corresponding classes in this country; and into the influence of such instruction on manufacturing and other industries at home and abroad.

The Samuelson Report of 1884 concluded that Britain was still the leading industrial nation, and that there were several examples of scientific and technical instruction in the major industrial centres and elsewhere. Nevertheless it warned of superior educational provision in some other European countries: for example elementary education in Germany, and some adult instruction in Belgium and France.[23] This warning was repeated in the Bryce Report of 1895 which advised that 'Not a few commentators have dilated upon the disadvantages from which young Englishmen suffer in industry and commerce owing to the superior preparation of their competitors in several countries of continental Europe.'[24]

Both the Samuelson and Bryce Reports placed the development of scientific and technical education within the broader context of administrative educational reform. But, as Guagnini has shown with specific reference to the training of mechanical engineers in England between 1850 and 1914, there were two other fundamental problems to be overcome. The first, given the success of British industry so far, and the apparent connection of such success with practical rather than academic preparation, was a preference both among employers and engineers themselves, for on-the-job training. The second was the reluctance of some of the most prestigious institutions of higher education to grant degrees in engineering.[25]

Culture

Although both economic and educational factors may be adduced to explain British shortcomings in the second, and subsequent, industrial revolutions, the most influential analyses have drawn upon the wider themes of culture and ideology. Prominent amongst such explanations has been Martin Wiener's, *English Culture and the Decline of the Industrial Spirit, 1850–1980*, which begins with the unequivocal statement that 'The leading problem of modern British history is the explanation of economic decline'.[26]

The explanation for the deleterious effect of British (and particularly English) culture upon the nation's economic performance is as follows. Though Britain was the first industrial and urban country of modern times, heavily populated and crisscrossed by railways and roads, the most powerful groups in Victorian society still clung to the serenity and trappings of a rural way of life. The values and society of county and shire continued to predominate over those of city and town. In contrast to those countries in which industrialization took place at a later stage, where the process was more rapid, and even directed by central government, in Britain industrialization was both protracted and haphazard. In consequence, while its ultimate economic and social effects, as the majority of inhabitants moved from field to factory and from village to town, were considerable, no commensurate radical change occurred in respect of constitutional or political power. The industrial bourgeoisie were smoothly assimilated into the existing ruling elite, and many of the entrepreneurs who had pioneered the modernization of Britain acquired land, titles and a conservative frame of mind. As Wiener observed, 'old values and patterns of behaviour lived on within the new, whose character was thus profoundly modified'.[27]

Many authors and cultural critics who witnessed the encroachment of the 'dark satanic mills' across the 'green and pleasant land', for example William Blake and Charles Dickens, Matthew Arnold and John Ruskin, deplored the effects of industrialization upon the human condition, and in so doing provided a justification for the continuance of the rural ideal. One particular means of giving educational expression to this ideal – rural, classical and liberal – was the boys' public school. In such schools sons of landed society, of the new entrepreneurs, and of the burgeoning professional classes, could be forged together into a new ruling elite. The purpose of such schools was to produce Christian gentlemen, not leaders of further industrial and commercial revolutions. Their curricula were not based upon the wonders of new technology, nor the discipline of the counting house; indeed they took little account of the modern world at all. Classics – the study of the ancient languages, culture and values of Greece and Rome – provided the core curriculum, justified as a means of mental training, of social distinction, and of inspiration for those who would be called to public service, at home or overseas, in the greatest empire the world had ever seen. These schools, with their anti-industrial values and assumptions, not only continued into the twentieth century largely unchanged, but also supplied a model for the maintained secondary schools established after the Education Act of 1902.

According to this cultural analysis, the main problems that were to affect the economic performance of Britain from 1851 until the present day were not to be found in particular failures to modernize this or that industry, but rather in the dominant social and educational values of the second half of the nineteenth century – in the liberalism of John Stuart Mill, the nostalgic medievalism of William Morris, and the idea of a university as expressed by John Henry Newman. In the minds of such men 'The industrial and the technical were widely seen as inevitably dehumanising. The basis of a continuing, educational anti-industrialism, anti-vocationalism, had been laid.'[28] In consequence, the elite educational institutions of England, both at secondary and tertiary level, concerned themselves with 'pure' rather than 'applied' subjects, with classics and physics rather than with accountancy and engineering.

This cultural explanation for economic decline, as outlined in the work of Wiener and Barnett, may be criticized from at least three standpoints. The first is that in spite of the fame (and, on occasion, of the fortunes) of the liberal literati, an essential entrepreneurial ethos – hard work, self-help, thrift and profit – predominated in Victorian Britain. The second is to set the names of such champions of science and technology as Thomas Huxley, Lyon Playfair and Bernhard Samuelson against those of Mill, Morris and Newman, and to acknowledge that the later nineteenth century did witness widespread and significant developments in educational provision for scientific and technological study. As Hennock has observed:

> There can be no mistaking the willingness by the 1890s of the English university colleges both in London and the provinces to include technology in their programme of teaching and research . . . [after 1890] . . . the State had not merely begun through the Treasury to finance the universities and university colleges on a regular basis, but in the form of local government had either taken over or founded technical colleges in practically every English city.[29]

A third critique of the cultural thesis may be developed from Rubinstein's argument that even in 1851 British economic power was not so much industrial as financial and commercial, an argument buttressed with substantial evidence as to the concentration of wealth in London. Rubinstein also supplies evidence from a sample of eight boys' public schools, to question the hypothesis that it was in such schools that sons of the entrepreneurial classes were taught to despise their origins and to seek new fields of employment. Rubinstein divides the occupations of entrants to these schools, and their fathers, into three broad categories: land, professionals, business, this latter category conflating his earlier crucial distinction between industry on the one hand and commerce and finance on the other. He shows the predominance of sons of the professional classes (only at Eton and Harrow were there substantial cohorts from the landed classes) and that there was a natural tendency for sons to follow their fathers' occupations. Only 36 per cent of entrants were sons of business men, and (although tracing subsequent occupations proved to be more difficult than identifying those of fathers) at least 57.9 per cent, and probably more than 70 per cent of these sons, themselves took up business careers.[30]

Rubinstein's work may, in turn, be criticized, both for its refusal to acknowledge the statistical (and other highly visible) evidence of relative British economic decline since 1945, and for the harmful effects of the imposition of immediate financial priorities and goals upon British industry, where accountants rather than engineers hold sway. But it does provide an important historical perspective to explain why, in the 1980s and 1990s, the demise of the British industrial base was viewed with apparent equanimity by government and the City alike.

In the first half of the twentieth century avoidance of revolution coupled with success in two World Wars combined to confirm the supremacy of the institutions, hierarchies and values of British society. Though the working classes now had a representative party in Parliament, neither of the minority Labour governments of 1924 and 1929 could provide solutions to the chronic problems of poverty and unemployment which characterized so much of the inter-war period. In 1931, faced with yet another financial crisis, the response of the Labour leader, Ramsay MacDonald, was to form a 'National' government in which Conservatives predominated. Radical central direction of economic and social life, including that of schools, for the purpose of promoting national superiority, was tainted by the obvious dangers of the implementation of such policies by Fascist and Communist dictators alike. Freedom remained an important watchword, and legislation to provide compulsory part-time education for all those not engaged in full-time study, up to age 16 under the 1918 Act, and to age 18 under the 1944 Act, came to nothing.

Education reflected these continuities. Secondary grammar schools continued to flourish, while technical schools eked out a subordinate, tiny and often short-lived existence. The majority of pupils, even after the widespread adoption of the ideal of secondary education for all, learned in their elementary and secondary modern schools to know their place in the economic, social and cultural hierarchies of the twentieth century, as their forebears had done in the nineteenth. There was no parity of esteem among the three types of secondary schools – grammar, technical and modern – with which Britain entered the second half of the twentieth century, and nothing to compare with the scientific and technical education available at secondary level in the schools of such economic rivals as France and Germany. Expense was one reason why technical schools failed to materialize in substantial numbers; another was the concern among many educationists that technical aptitudes were less easily determined at age 11 than those of general intelligence.

Understandably, but with respect to economic performance probably unfortunately, educational reform in this period concentrated upon organizational matters, rather than upon those of nature and quality. The abolition of tripartism and the achievement of comprehensive secondary education diverted attention away from other issues – notably those of standards and curricula. General Certificate of Education examinations, at both Ordinary and Advanced levels seemed to confirm that the purpose of schooling was to identify and reward an elite who could demonstrate ability in academic subjects. For the majority of pupils there was a clear dichotomy between school and work: the second being the means of escape from the first. At the beginning of the 1960s more than 70 per cent of pupils departed their schools in England and Wales without having sat a school-leaving examination.

Central direction

The introduction of the Certificate of Secondary Education from 1965 provided both a publicly recognized examination for the majority of secondary school pupils, and a further means of comparing standards of attainment with competitor countries. Although such comparisons must always be treated with caution, several studies led to the inescapable conclusion that general standards were too low. Research by Prais and Wagner and by Sanderson revealed that in the first half of the 1980s some 60 per cent of West German school leavers secured the equivalent of five or more GCE 'O'-level passes as compared to only 27 per cent in England and Wales. A mere 10 per cent of German pupils left school with fewer than the equivalent of five CSE passes, whereas in England and Wales more than a third left with only one or two CSE passes. Specific studies of attainment in mathematics revealed a similar picture. By the end of the 1980s only a third of 16-year-olds in Britain obtained the equivalent of an 'O'-level pass, in contrast to more than two-thirds in France, Germany and Japan.[31] One justification for the introduction under the Education Reform Act of 1988 of a National Curriculum and national testing was to raise standards to match those of competitor countries.

Though it may be argued that high standards in basic subjects, rather than in those specifically related to technological, commercial and industrial employment, are the proper purpose of schools, at various stages in the twentieth century schools had been urged to tailor their curricula to the needs of local employment. For example the Hadow Report of 1926 advised that a practical bias might be introduced into the third and fourth years of classes in modern schools 'after careful consideration of local conditions and upon the advice of persons connected with the local industries'.[32] While school curricula remained under the direction of local authorities, or of the schools themselves, such advice as to the need to involve the business community in curriculum design went largely unheeded. In 1963 the report of the Newsom Committee on the education of pupils aged between 13 and 16 of average and less than average ability, once again drew attention to the importance of practical and vocational subjects in the school curriculum. In the same year, Harold Wilson, in a speech to the annual conference of the Labour Party at Scarborough, pledged his commitment to a new Britain, one in which improved education and economic performance would go hand in hand. This would require

> a revolution in our attitude to education, not only higher education but at every level . . . The Britain that is going to be forged in the white heat of this revolution will be no place for restrictive practices or for outdated methods on either side of industry. We shall need a totally new attitude to the problems of apprenticeship, of training and re-training for skill.[33]

Some thirteen years later Wilson's concerns were echoed by his successor as Labour leader, James Callaghan, when in his speech at Ruskin College he urged that pupils should be properly equipped to 'do a job of work', and that too many of those who completed higher education had 'no desire or intention of joining industry'. From 1979 rhetoric was replaced by action with the advent to power of the Conservative government of Margaret Thatcher. A series of curriculum reforms ensued: notably the Technical and Vocational Education Initiative and the Certificate of Pre-Vocational Education. Many of these initiatives were originally fiercely resisted by professional educators, teachers and others, who feared both a loss of professional control over the curriculum, and the general subordination of education to training and specifically to the vocational and capitalist ethos of David Young and the Manpower Services Commission. Though the Education Reform Act of 1988 represented the restoration of school initiatives to the Department of Education and Science, its radical programme, coupled with the manner of its implementation, also provoked considerable controversy.

While general issues about curriculum and standards in schools have been identified as one area in which economic performance may be promoted by educational reform, a second concern relates to the vocational education and training of those in the 16 to 19 age range and beyond. While in other countries young people, on leaving school, were required to engage in a period of formal vocational training which led to recognized qualifications as a condition of employment, in the United Kingdom no such expectation existed. This situation was exacerbated in the period after 1944 by the failure to develop technical schools or to implement the provisions for county colleges. As in previous ages there was no lack of awareness of the problem, and the needs of industry for trained scientists and technologists were addressed in a series of reports: the Percy Report into higher technological education of 1945, and the Barlow Report on 'Scientific Manpower' of the following year; a White Paper on technical education of 1956, and another on industrial training in 1962. But, in spite of reports such as these which emphasised the need for higher standards and for more co-operation between academic institutions and employers, apprenticeship remained the basic form of training. Although some large firms provided systematic and worthwhile programmes of study, in many cases apprenticeship was a condition of employment rather than a guarantee of genuine training.

The Industrial Training Act of 1964 recognized that in the interests of national economic performance it was unwise to leave such training solely in the hands of employers who might justifiably decline to invest heavily in the preparation of apprentices who might subsequently leave their employ for posts in other, even rival, firms. But narrow interests, both at employer and at union level, and the reluctance of successive governments to intervene in an apprenticeship system which could be traced back at least to the Statute of Artificers of 1563, meant that while such systems were modernized or replaced in competitor countries, in Britain apprenticeship fell into desuetude without an effective alternative being devised to replace it. In the middle of the 1960s there were some 240,000 apprentices in manufacturing industry. Numbers fell to 140,000 in 1974 and a mere 54,000 in 1989.[34]

Nevertheless, since the 1980s, there have been several initiatives, emanating both from the business and educational worlds, to forge stronger links between the two. Chairs and research in higher education have been sponsored by the business community, while a recent survey indicated that 92 per cent of secondary schools and 56 per cent of primary schools had links with local business.[35]

The industrial training boards established under the 1964 Act failed to provide the necessary basis for vocational education, and a new chapter began with the creation of the Manpower Services Commission in 1973. Nevertheless, the decade of the 1970s was as problematic as those which had gone before. In 1980 expenditure on educational training by employers in West Germany was calculated at £7 billion as opposed to £2.5 billion for the United Kingdom. This gap was not made up by contributions from public funds. In 1978 the percentage of public expenditure on education devoted to vocational training in the United Kingdom was only 8.1 per cent, as opposed to 16 per cent in the European Community as a whole.[36]

Conservative initiatives of the 1980s sought to address two problems – youth unemployment and low training levels. The Youth Training Scheme (YTS) of 1983 which replaced the Youth Opportunities Programme (YOP) introduced some five years before, provided a year's course including work experience, off-the-job training and an allowance of £25 per week. A two-year scheme was inaugurated in 1986, with more emphasis upon competencies in core, personal and occupational skills. Such schemes were urgently needed. In 1974, 61 per cent of all 16-year-olds were employed; by 1984 the figure had fallen to 18 per cent.[37] YOP and YTS kept youngsters off the dole and off the streets, and provided a bridge between school and work. Critics, however, complained of the cost, the use by employers of these trainees as a source of cheap labour, and the absence of recognized exit qualifications.

By 1992 a new framework for vocational training had been created. This comprised the National Council for Vocational Qualifications, the Training Agency, and more than eighty employer-led Training and Enterprise Councils. Whether the new framework will cure Britain's traditional shortage of skilled employees, or whether it represents yet another package of short-term measures, remains to be seen. On the one hand it could be argued that, whatever the shortcomings of individual training initiatives, since 1979 the United Kingdom has moved significantly in the direction of an entrepreneurial state, and one in which the relevance of high standards of education and training to improved economic performance has, at last, been grasped. Critics, however, have maintained that while, once again, the nature and extent of the vocational training problem has been appreciated, unco-ordinated and piecemeal solutions have been supplied, so that in relative terms the skills gap between the United Kingdom and other countries has widened rather than narrowed. One commentator has concluded that

> Even by the end of the 1980s, after years of trial and error, Britain's workforce remained under-educated, under-trained and under-qualified. One-third of school leavers had no useful qualifications to show for eleven years of compulsory education; one-half of those employed had no educational qualifications equivalent to the old GCE 'O' level; and two-thirds of the workforce had no

worthwhile vocational qualifications. Furthermore, just over one-half (two-thirds in manufacturing) of the workforce received no systematic training in 1987, fewer than one in three employers had a training plan or training budget, only one in five evaluated the benefits of training in any way, while only one in ten had formal training targets for the whole workforce.[38]

Such skill shortages, particularly where complemented by amateurish management and lack of investment in research and development, on occasion have been instrumental not only in generating low productivity in comparison with other countries, but also products whose design, quality, reliability and delivery have been found wanting in the face of international competition.

CONCLUSION

Five conclusions may be drawn.

The first is that the historical perspective indicates the complexity of the relationship between education and economic performance. There is no constant relationship between the two and, indeed, at times, apparently little relationship, if any, at all. Economic success depends upon a variety of factors – some of which may be described as being essentially economic, while others are of a broad cultural nature, and others again specific to what happens in schools. Connections between education and economic performance in terms of investment (as opposed to consumption) may be represented partly in ideals and values, in subjects and standards. Ideals and values, subjects and standards, are reflected in the attitudes and priorities of teachers, pupils and parents, of schools and curricula, and of employers and governments.

From the standpoint of history it seems clear that many English educational institutions, and the overall system in which they have been located, have had a negative attitude towards vocational education, except as a preparation for traditionally high-status occupations and professions. Two basic manifestations of this negative attitude in the second half of the twentieth century may be identified. The first is that secondary technical schools were never developed in substantial numbers, so that the supposed parity of esteem between three types of secondary schools in the years after the Second World War remained pure fiction. The second is demonstrated by the shortage of technical, vocational and commercial courses leading to GCE Advanced level qualifications, and the low status of education and training provided for those in the 16–19 age range who neither wished to follow academic subjects nor, immediately, to proceed to higher education.

While cultural explanations of British economic decline, such as those of Barnett and Wiener, must be subjected to rigorous scrutiny and substantial caveats, it is clear that the traditional institutions and hierarchies of the medieval and early modern periods – monarchy, aristocracy, Parliament and Church – were challenged and reformed, but not overthrown by the industrial and commercial revolutions of the nineteenth century. The same was true of the medieval educational system. Though new universities were founded in the nineteenth century, universities which in many instances had close connections with the industrial and commercial worlds, and though secondary schooling for all was achieved in the twentieth century, the ancient universities of Oxford and Cambridge and medieval schools such as Eton and Westminster, with their historic buildings, traditional aura and associated anti-industrial ethos, continued to be the most prestigious in the land.

One consequence of these continuities, in the state, society and in education, was that although the relationship between inadequate general and vocational education and poor economic performance was identified by a succession of critics from the 1860s, and particularly during two World Wars, reforms were at best piecemeal and contradictory. Avoidance of substantial reform, however, should not simply be laid at the door of the Establishment. Governments, local authorities, employers, trade unionists, universities, teachers, parents and pupils have all been resistant to change. Such resistance reflects the survival of nineteenth-century social and cultural divisions, and the ability of those who have traditionally used the education system to promote their own ends and those of their children, to continue to do so. It also reflects the deep conservatism of the political Left, including that of trade union leaders, as much as any reaction from the political Right. Indeed since 1979, in education as in other spheres of British life, the term 'radical Right' has been generally and accurately applied.

Given such conservatism and divisions, attention must be focused on the role of central government. As the chapter on 'Control' indicated, in modern times central government's role in education has been reluctant and partial. Its prime goal has been economy of expenditure rather than investment through education in the economy. In consequence, in the twentieth century, as in the nineteenth, education in the United Kingdom, and particularly within England, has lacked the coherent vision and plan which would have united the various partners in a national economic goal – in this case the achievement of a better educated and skilled workforce for the purpose of raising the general standard of living of all its inhabitants. The Committee of the Privy Council, established in 1839, was a most imperfect instrument, and since that date successive central authorities have failed to promote the economic well-being of the nation by means of education. Indeed, it could be argued that the greatest progress has been made during periods when major rivals arose to the Education Department, as from 1853 with the rivalry between the Education Department at Whitehall and the Department of Science and Art at South Kensington.

While the demise of the Science and Art Department in 1899, however, might have been welcomed by those who hoped to see a more unified direction of general and vocational education under the Board of Education, twentieth-century developments, whether under the Board or the Ministry, showed such hopes to have been illusory. The redesignation of the Ministry of Education as the Department of Education and Science in 1964 indicated some awareness of the 'world that had been lost' or neglected, but it took the challenge of the Manpower Services Commission, created in 1973, particularly under the direction of David Young, to stimulate activity in redefining the relationship between schooling and work. The National Commission's proposals for a new Department for Education and Training and the establishment in 1995 of the Department for Education and Employment may be seen as a logical development in respect of the perceived need to bring the worlds of school and work even closer together, but there is a danger that traditional hierarchies in respect of subjects and education and training, may be reinforced rather than weakened by such a creation. At institutional level the traditional unwillingness, or inability, to create substantial numbers of high-status scientific and technical schools appears to be as visible in the 1990s as it was in the 1890s or 1940s. Within schools, higher educational institutions and the workplace, the progress and standing of National Vocational Qualifications will be crucial.

Finally, it is important to note that while the relationship between education and economic performance is usually approached in terms of what must be done to education to meet the needs of commerce and industry, other perspectives must be applied. In the 1980s and 1990s it would appear that, in spite of many adversities, the educational world, both in schools and particularly in higher education, has shown a capacity for adaptation and growth which could well provide an example for other sectors of the society and of the economy.

NOTES

1. McCarthy, 1985, 5.
2. *Sunday Times*, 7 March 1993.
3. *The Times*, 5 March 1993.
4. *Sunday Times*, 7 March 1993.
5. *Sunday Times*, 28 March 1993.
6. Rubinstein, 1993, 25.
7. Randlesome *et al*, 1990, 190.
8. Minshull, 1990, 74.
9. *National Commission Report*, 1993, 18.
10. *National Commission Report*, 1993, 31.
11. Hough, 1987, 56–9.
12. Antal, 1990, 21–3.
13. Steedman and Green, 1993, 45.
14. Randlesome *et al*, 1990, 202.
15. *National Commission Report*, 1993, 247.
16. *National Commission Report*, 1993, 35–6.
17. Mitchell and Deane, 1962, 338–62.
18. Floud and McCloskey, 1981, I, 110.
19. Mathias, 1983, 124.
20. Barnett, 1972, 94.
21. Barnett, 1972, 84.
22. Rubinstein, 1993, 8–9.
23. Maclure, 1969, 121–2.
24. Quoted in Maclure, 1969, 148.
25. Guagnini, 1993, 16–17.
26. Wiener, 1981, 3.

27. Wiener, 1981, 7.
28. Benson and Silver, 1991, 2.
29. Hennock, 1990, 330–1.
30. Rubinstein, 1993, 115–21.
31. Aldcroft, 1992, 41.
32. Quoted in Maclure, 1969, 186.
33. Quoted in Bell, Fowler and Little, 1973, 192–4.
34. Aldcroft, 1992, 58.
35. *National Commission Report*, 1993, 168.
36. Aldcroft, 1992, 62–3.
37. Roberts *et al*, 1988, 23.
38. Aldcroft, 1992, 72–3.

SUGGESTED READING

Aldcroft, D. (1992) *Education, Training and Economic Performance, 1944–1990.*
Cotgrove, S. F. (1958) *Technical Education and Social Change.*
Rubinstein, W. D. (1993) *Capitalism, Culture and Decline in Britain, 1750–1990.*
Sanderson, M. (1972) *The Universities and British Industry, 1850–1970.*
West, E. G. (1975) *Education and the Industrial Revolution.*
Wiener, M. J. (1981) *English Culture and the Decline of the Industrial Spirit, 1850–1980.*
Worswick, G. (ed.) (1985) *Education and Economic Performance.*

SEVEN

Consumers

CURRENT ISSUES

The terms 'consumers' and 'producers', in common with those of consumption and production, have generally been applied to economic life. Consumers, though the word retains particular connotations in respect of eating and drinking (especially in immoderate or eager fashion) may be defined as those who purchase or otherwise make use of goods or services.

In recent years in England the term 'consumers' has been applied to a much wider range of circumstances than previously. Margaret Thatcher, Secretary of State for Education 1970–74, and Prime Minister 1979–90, sought to revitalize the economy and culture by the introduction of market forces into virtually all spheres of life, and by emphasising the interests of consumers as opposed to those of producers. The logic behind such policies was that the market distributes resources in the most effective manner, since each individual is the best judge of her or his own interests. Accordingly, state monopolies were dismantled and privatized, trade unions emasculated and their wildcat strikes and restrictive practices outlawed, the powers and privileges of the older professions abolished. Under the new system consumer choice would decide which schools or hospitals flourished or declined, just as consumer choice decided which manufacturer, retailer or airline flourished, and which went to the wall. Basic standards, however, would be guaranteed by a series of consumer charters.

In the judgement of Margaret Thatcher and of many of her colleagues, the world of education had acquired a producer-dominated ethos that was damaging to the true interests of the consumers of education. Too much power was in the hands of the local education authorities and of the teacher unions. Too much money was being spent on administration. Too much emphasis was being placed on social engineering – anti-racism and anti-sexism – and not enough upon the traditional values of hard work and high standards. Too many of the consumers of state education were getting a poor deal, as pupils emerged from eleven years of formal schooling with deplorable standards of basic literacy and numeracy and little to show in terms of formal qualifications.

Accordingly, the role of the producers of education – local education authorities, teachers (particularly teacher unions), teacher training institutions – was diminished, and that of the consumers increased. The abolition of the Greater London Council (GLC) was followed by the abolition of the Inner London Education Authority (ILEA); the sale of council houses by the opting out of schools. Teachers' associations and unions were excluded from government counsels, and the tenure of university teachers revoked. Choice and diversity in education were increased by a variety of means: assisted places, city technology colleges, grant-maintained schools, maintained schools; devolution of powers to schools and to their governing bodies; charters which guaranteed parents the right of access to information about schools, including examination results and the right to express preferences for schools for their children; the open enrolment of pupils so that successful schools would flourish and unpopular schools be eliminated.

At least three major issues arise from such policies. Who are the consumers of education? Do their interests, and those of the producers, conflict or coincide? What are the effects of the application of market principles to education?

Consumers come in various shapes and sizes. Pupils and students are in the front line. Those aged between 5 and 16 are consumers under compulsion: their presence in classrooms is required by law. Older students may bring market forces into play in quite specific ways – choosing institutions and courses on a strict criterion of value for money. Which institutions and courses will be the cheapest in terms of fees and living expenses? Which will provide most chance of success in terms of levels of qualification, of subsequent employability and earning power? Parents are consumers. Some pay directly for the education of their children, in pre-school playgroups and nursery classes, in independent schools, in further and higher education. Even for those parents whose children attend maintained schools for which no fees are levied, there may be other costs – in uniforms, transport, forgoing of earnings, etc. Indeed a creeping level of direct parental financial assistance for state schools is apparent. Whilst parents have for long contributed towards what might be called 'extras' – the purchase of a school minibus, the construction of a swimming pool – there is evidence that money is now being supplied directly for basic services. For example, a survey conducted by the National Confederation of Parent-Teacher Associations and reported in 1991, showed that parents were annually finding at least £55 million from their own pockets to provide books and equipment for lessons in National Curriculum subjects.[1] In the following year parents of pupils at a Warwickshire comprehensive school were being asked to contribute an annual sum of £40 to supplement its budget.[2] In 1995, as central government funding levels for schools were further reduced, direct contributions were sought from parents in order to retain the services of teachers whose jobs had been put at risk.

There are two distinct views on such direct parental contributions to the financing of state schools. The first is that free education is a right, free because the nation as a whole accepts in principle that all children are entitled to a good education whatever the financial circumstances of their parents, and supplies the appropriate finance by the payment of national and local taxes. The opposite position is that schools will be conducted with the greatest efficiency if parental consumers have a direct financial stake, however modest, in their operation.

Educational institutions are themselves consumers. Universities consume some of the products of secondary schools, which in term consume the products of primary schools. Attention is sometimes drawn to that relationship in the context of dissatisfaction with the quality of products from the previous stage. Secondary school teachers complain that too many primary school pupils arrive with deficiencies in basic skills, for example with reading levels well below that appropriate for their age. University tutors regret a decline in standards of entrants, and in the rigour of certain 'A'-level courses, declaring that in some degree programmes much of the first year is spent on 'remedial' work.

Employers are consumers. Their often-quoted concerns about the poor attainment levels, inappropriate qualifications and attitudes of school leavers have been legion. In 1995 the Japanese electrical manufacturing giant, Panasonic, had six apprenticeships available at one of its British factories. From more than 200 applicants, only three were deemed to be suitably qualified, and recruited.[3] Finally, the nation, society at large, is a consumer of education. The whole community benefits insofar as the products of the formal educational process are law-abiding, self-reliant and hard-working, and suffers when they are not.

One major difference between consumers in education and consumers in the sphere of goods and services, is that many consumers in education also have roles as producers. The purchaser of a television set or of an airline ticket is not likely also to be engaged in supplying televisions or air transport services to others. But the roles of producers and consumers in education are often closely interlocked. Pupils and students do not just consume education, they also play a significant part in their own education, and in the education of their peers. Indeed, one of the major aims of the formal educational process is to promote the capacity for self-education. The role of parents as producers of education is fundamental. Not only are they solely responsible for the production of the raw materials – those to be educated – it is parents who initially, and subsequently, supply their children with many attributes and skills – speech, manners, principles, expectations. Indeed schools may consider themselves to be the consumers of parental products. In 1991 Peter Dawson, General Secretary to the Professional Association of Teachers, expressed the view that 'Almost every child who is a problem in school comes from a problem home. It is time for teachers to draw attention to this. There are now over a million single-parent families in this country and they are causing tremendous problems in schools.'[4]

Educational institutions, as indicated above, clearly fulfil the roles of producers and consumers. The secondary school acts as a consumer of the products of primary schools, but is itself in the role of producer in respect of further and higher education, and of employers. Employers, too, are producers of education. It can be argued that if recruits from school are of poor quality that is to some extent because English employers themselves are frequently poorly qualified in comparison with some of their foreign contemporaries and competitors, and have placed too little value upon education both for their recruits and for their current employees.

Although the commitment of English employers to education and training has frequently been criticized, a survey of training in the United Kingdom in 1986–87 indicated that of the £33 billion devoted to this purpose, £18 billion was contributed by employers as opposed to £8 billion by the trainees themselves and £7 billion by government.[5]

The nation, society at large, is also a producer as well as a consumer of education. Such education is produced in a multiplicity of ways – for example through the media, politics, the arts and sport. Central government has both a specific and a general role as a producer of education, specific in that it bears ultimate responsibility for the formal educational system of the nation, and general in respect of its wider promotion of ideology and legislation in national life. Although, in recent years, central government has sought to depict local education authorities as producers of education and itself as a consumer, or even a disinterested party, there can be no doubt that central government is the major single producer of education in the country. Indeed one of the major criticisms of some educational consumers is that central government has paid insufficient attention to its role as an educational producer.

Do the interests of consumers of education conflict? If a commodity is in short supply then not all would-be consumers can be satisfied. For example, if the numbers of places in higher education are fewer than the numbers of applicants, then competition will ensue and the interests of these potential consumers may be in direct opposition. A broader interest may, however, be served if such competition raises the standards of all participants, including those who are unsuccessful. On the other hand conflict between consumer interests may be avoided by establishing a standard deemed to be suitable for admission to higher education and guaranteeing places for all who reached it. Conflict may also arise between the interests of different types of consumers of education. For example, it can be argued that all pupils should, in their own interests, be educated to be ambitious and outgoing, determined to improve their position and status in life. Some employers, on the other hand, may prefer sections of their workforce to have quite the opposite qualities, and to be content with a humdrum and unambitious existence.

In terms of general policy and market ideology the real interests of the immediate consumers of education, pupils and students, might best be met by allowing them, or their parents, a voucher equal in value to the fees required for attendance at the most expensive independent school. All pupils would then have the means to attend independent schools or to provide state schools with the resources equal to those deemed to be necessary by the most expensive independent schools. On the other hand such an increase in educational expenditure might be considered unnecessary by central government as a consumer of education. If employers and the state can function with a relatively small percentage of well-educated persons, a percentage produced by current funding levels, it might be deemed to be in their interests as consumers to provide expensive education only for a minority, by means of a selection procedure and an assisted places scheme.

One particular example of a conflict of consumer interest occurred over the abolition of the ILEA. This abolition took place under the terms of the Education

Reform Act of 1988, and was justified on the grounds of consumer interests. Central government declared that the ILEA was too expensive, too concerned with non-educational issues, and too tolerant of low standards. A ballot of one of the most important groups of consumers, however, parents of children attending ILEA schools, showed an overwhelming vote in favour of the continuation of this particular education producer.

Another example of conflicting consumer demands occurred over the curriculum. Central government in its consumer role decided that a compulsory, subject-based curriculum, with regular national assessment, would be the most efficient and cost-effective means of raising educational standards, and of providing all consumers with information about the quality of schools. Some pupils and parents, however, and many advocates of the application of market principles to education, regarded a National Curriculum as central government acting in a producer role and denying consumers the right to express their own curricular preferences.

There is also a concern that central government, in its role as producer, has rigged the market, for example by granting extra funding to city technology colleges and grant-maintained schools. Such an action may be justified on the grounds that diverse institutions must be created so that real choice can subsequently ensue. In the immediate term, however, such rigging of the market may mean that other schools are thereby deprived of funds to the extent that the very safety of their pupils is put at risk. A survey carried out by the National Union of Teachers reported that a quarter of state schools in England and Wales, some 6,000, had been forced to close dangerously decrepit buildings on their sites to protect pupils. Even so, in 20 per cent of schools at least one teacher or child had recently suffered injury or illness as the direct result of the poor state of the premises.[6]

Finally, what have been the effects of the introduction of market principles and consumer interests into education? Some elements have been beneficial: the greater involvement of parents and other consumers on school governing bodies; the application of measures of accountability at all stages in the educational process. But it is also clear that the roles of producers and consumers cannot be totally separated, and that it is the educational producers, in the shape of schools and universities, rather than the consumers, in the shape of parents and students, who have the ultimate power of choice. Indeed, since the introduction of the Education Reform Act of 1988 the effectiveness of parental choice of (or expression of preference for) schools appears to have declined rather than improved. In 1992 some 94 per cent of parents secured the first choice of secondary school for their children. In 1993 the figure fell to 90 per cent.[7] This conclusion is confirmed by a recent study from Scotland.

> The evidence from a decade of open enrolment in Scotland suggests that parental choice has led to an inefficient use of resources, widening disparities between schools, increased social segregation and threats to equality of educational opportunity.
>
> Although there have been gainers as well as losers, the balance sheet suggests that parental choice has been a 'negative sum game' in which the gains achieved

by some pupils have been more than offset by the losses incurred by others and by the community as a whole.

It is likely that the outcomes of open enrolment in England will be even more problematic.[8]

Recent legislation has naturally increased the expectation of parents in respect of choice. For example in 1988 some 10,500 parents appealed over school admissions; by 1990–91 the figure had risen to 25,000.[9] Such consumer expectations cannot be met by a limited increase in the enrolment of a few schools, but only by the provision of good and effective schools for all.

HISTORICAL PERSPECTIVES

If the education system itself stands accused of being producer dominated so, too, does the history of education as a discipline. This stems, in part, from a basic neglect of the theme of consumers, but it also reflects difficulties with evidence. Historical perspectives on consumers are not easily determined, for while the producers and providers of education have left considerable testimony as to their role and work – for example in government and institutional archives – historical evidence as to the role of consumers is more difficult to locate. This is especially so in respect of members of the working class, and of females of all classes. While occasional autobiographies and diaries may furnish particular and revealing individual insights, the existence and survival of such material is haphazard in the extreme.

Nevertheless, the consumer's role in education has been an important one. It received particular expression in the form of the tutor, who was an established feature in many households from the sixteenth to eighteenth centuries, though later to be supplemented, and even supplanted, by that of the governess. In such situations the provider of education was quite definitely at the service of his or her employer – the consumer – who might exercise very considerable control over the content, methods and outcomes of the educational process. In such instances education would be tailored specifically to individual needs and requirements.

Gardner has argued, with specific reference to working-class consumers, that the history of education all too often reflects

> an orientation which looks overwhelmingly to the study of institutions and of official policy . . . In this perspective, the concept of 'education' is narrowed to a known and agreed facility, to a neutral process that is simply 'done' to people, both for their individual benefit and for the good of society as a whole. In so far as the notions of power and conflict impinge on this view at all, they are restricted to accounts of the competition between rival institutional suppliers of an essentially similar and straightforward product.[10]

Historical generalizations about consumers of education are fraught with difficulty. Nevertheless, it can be stated with some certainty that, overall, the children of wealthy parents had more choice in matters of education than did those of the poor, and boys more than girls. During the nineteenth century consumer choice increased substantially for more affluent parents. This was the result of several factors. The very growth in population meant that there was a commensurate increase in the numbers (and types) of schools. Day pupils in urban areas were more likely to be presented with a choice of schools within easy walking distance. At the same time, boarding schools mushroomed, particularly in rural areas made nationally accessible by the proliferation of railway links. For those parents who could afford the fees there was a bewildering variety of private schools, both for boys and for girls. Indeed, the Taunton Commissioners estimated their numbers in the 1860s to be in excess of 10,000, as compared to some 2,000 non-classical, and 700 classical, endowed schools.

The great weakness of private, as opposed to public or endowed, schools was that they were too frequently dependent upon the health, longevity, teaching skill and business acumen of a single individual. Schools of a public nature customarily had a board of governors, managers or trustees whose principal duties were to ensure that the terms of founders' deeds or statutes were obeyed, to appoint the master or mistress, and to ensure continuity.

The numerous advertisements of those who ran private schools provide some evidence as to their perceptions of consumers' requirements in such areas as curriculum, care and control. One of the distinguishing features of the private, as opposed to the public, boys' schools was that they were generally more flexible in matters of curriculum. Another was that the pupils were not left to their own devices, but under the care of a master at all times, and a third the greater attention paid to home comforts in the private schools. These concerns ran counter to the widely held belief amongst providers, and some consumers, of boys' public schools, that it was the very spartan conditions of such schools and the freedom accorded to their pupils that produced the independence and manliness so desirable in an English gentleman.

H. A. Giffard, who reported on private schools in Surrey for the Taunton Commission, indicated consumer concerns:

> The accommodation, both in respect of day-rooms and sleeping-rooms is, in the upper class of private schools, with few exceptions, satisfactory. In fact the domestic arrangements are always looked after by the parents when they place a boy at a school, and these and the diet often form the sole objects of their attention. The proprietors of private boarding schools are generally very ready to show a visitor over their establishments, and are for the most part very proud of the extent and comfort of their houses. One of the boasts of the good boarding schools is that boys are treated as if they were at home.[11]

Another example of responsiveness to consumer demand was the publication of examination results. In the first half of the nineteenth century one of the major problems for parents as consumers was how to assess the relative academic merits of schools. From the 1860s league tables of results in middle-class examinations began to appear in the educational press. Examinations also helped schools to acquire particular identities by preparing boys for specific careers. In many cases such boys were following in their father's footsteps.

Nineteenth-century girls' schools for children from the wealthier classes in society were less easily categorized in terms of examination results or occupational grounds. Girls and women were excluded from many of the occupations and associated examinations available to men. Private arrangements predominated; the Taunton Commission found only twelve endowed grammar schools for girls in England and Wales. In girls' private schools family dimensions were frequently very strong indeed, and roles of consumer and producer often blurred. For example, a mother might take in other girls to teach alongside her own daughters and young sons.

Family arrangements and the blurring of consumer and producer roles also occurred in respect of private schools for the children of the working classes. Such private schools existed under a number of names and guises – dame schools, common day schools, private adventure schools. The Newcastle Commission, which reported in 1861, estimated that of the 2,213,694 children of the poorer classes in England and Wales, the names of more than a quarter, some 573,536, were on the books of private schools. These schools were supported by fees paid directly by working-class parents. It is also important to note that many of the parents of the 1,519,312 children whose names were on the books of public elementary societies paid a considerable proportion of the schools' income through school pence or other fee systems.

Since compulsory elementary schooling only began to be introduced from 1870, for most of the nineteenth century, as in previous ages, working-class parents, and their children, were able to choose whether to attend school or not. Even the public elementary schools, including those which received government grants, were heavily dependent upon the choices of their consumers. Of course, many types of pressure were placed upon children and parents to secure regular school attendance, from moral blackmail to homework and prize schemes but, as the logbooks of elementary schools regularly record, parental consumers kept their children from school for a variety of reasons: to help with the harvest; to look after younger siblings; to run errands. Consumer power was not only reflected in control over attendance, but also in the ultimate threat of removal of the pupil from the school. This threat might severely limit the freedom of teachers to impose punishment. As Harry Chester, assistant secretary to the Committee of the Privy Council on Education, 1840–58, wrote in 1860, 'Punish little Jack or Bill for any fault and immediately he will be transferred in state by his affronted mother to the opposition school.'[12]

On the other hand, working-class parents were frequently praised as good judges of their own best interests in education. As Assistant Commissioner Coode reported to the Newcastle Commission:

It is a subject of wonder how people so destitute of education as labouring parents commonly are, can be such just judges as they also commonly are of the effective qualifications of a teacher. Good school buildings and the apparatus of education are found for years to be practically useless and deserted, when, if a master chance to be appointed who understands his work, a few weeks suffice to make the fact known, and his school is soon filled, and perhaps found inadequate to the demand of the neighbourhood, and a separate girls' school or infants' school is soon found to be necessary.[13]

The willingness of so many working-class parents to pay higher fees to send their children to private, as opposed to public elementary, schools, was a matter of considerable contemporary concern and debate. Providers and supporters of the public elementary schools, which generally counted themselves to be superior to the private schools, explained the preference in terms of a desire to avoid their higher standards – academic, moral and disciplinary – and a mistaken belief among some parents that paying fees, of itself, conferred status and respectability. Whilst such factors might well have been important, private schools also responded to consumer needs and demands in a number of significant ways.

First amongst these was location. Private schools, being usually small and under the control of one teacher, were frequently situated in the teacher's house and easily accessible to the twenty or so pupils who might attend. Size in itself might also be seen as an advantage. A small school, with but a single class and room, would not have seemed so alien and intimidating as the purpose-built imitations of churches which represented the typical National Society school. Teachers in private schools, moreover, might be closer in many ways to parents. They were physically closer, and such proximity meant that they might also be friends and neighbours as well as teachers. They were spiritually closer, few having been through the mill of pupil teacher apprenticeship and training college, a process which removed many teachers in the public elementary schools from the class from which they had come, and transformed them into agents of control for the superior orders. Though teachers in private schools might themselves be young, they were less likely to be as young as the pupil teachers who constituted such a significant proportion of teachers in some public elementary schools, and whose attempts to enforce physical or other punishment upon pupils little younger than themselves were a frequent source of discontent. Physical and spiritual proximity meant that teachers in private schools were closely attuned to the demands and rhythms of working-class life. They were more likely to understand and accommodate the need for children to absent themselves from school, for shorter or longer periods, according to the fluctuating priorities of working-class existence. Teachers who demanded that children attended each and every day, irrespective of sickness at home, or the unemployment of a major breadwinner, would soon find themselves with no school at all.

Pupils in private schools were likely to be placed in smaller groups than in the public elementary schools, while individual, as opposed to class, methods of teaching, continued to predominate. This was often a matter of necessity rather than choice, given that a single class in a private school might contain children of quite varied ages, abilities and stages of development. In private schools children continued with the time-honoured method of learning their individual lessons, and then demonstrating such learning individually to the teacher. Such methods of learning enabled parents to exercise considerable control over the curriculum. Indeed they could prescribe what they wanted their children to learn. Immediate and specific goals could be set in private schools, unlike the public elementary schools in which, from 1862, teaching, learning and standards were tightly geared to the requirements of the Revised Code. Although it was obviously in the interests of the private teacher to keep children at school as long as possible, the best means of ensuring a ready stream of pupils was probably to satisfy consumers that their children could be taught what they needed to know in a speedy and effective manner.

Above all, private working-class schools belonged to the local community. They reflected the priorities and values of that community, not the alien impositions of Church and state. After 1870 they rapidly declined. Even the advocates of publicly maintained elementary schools, including Forster, the architect of the 1870 Act, attributed considerable importance to the direct payment of some part of the cost of schooling by parents. Free education, it was widely feared, would seriously diminish the important role of parents as consumers. These fears were soon realized. The provision of school boards from 1870, of compulsory attendance from 1880, and the ending of fees from 1891, conspired to deprive all but a minority of working-class consumers of an alternative form of elementary schooling. In the public elementary schools, control over curriculum and teaching methods, over attendance and discipline, belonged to central, local and voluntary bodies. In this period the rights of parents were replaced by duties. Compulsory school attendance, as under the 1870 and 1880 Acts, required parents to cause their children to attend schools in areas in which attendance bye-laws were in operation. Those who did not do so were subject to prosecution. Sandon's Act of 1876 placed the responsibility for causing a child to receive efficient elementary instruction in reading, writing and arithmetic upon the parents. When, at the turn of the century, central government relaxed its controls over such areas as curricula and teaching methods, power passed not to children and parents, but to another, and rapidly organizing, group of producers – the teachers.

Twentieth century

The demise of the working-class private school, and the failure to develop alternative means of popular educational control led to substantial tensions in many early twentieth-century schools. These tensions, which focused on such issues as curriculum and discipline, have led to contrasting analyses of the function of education at this time. On the one hand children who resisted school and schooling were criticized as hooligans who needed to change their lifestyles and attitudes, and to be supplied with different (and superior) cultural, intellectual and moral standards. An alternative interpretation was that children were rebels in a justifiable cause – the preservation of the independence and comradeship necessary for survival in the world in which they lived – and victims of misguided class oppression and social control. If, in the twentieth century, formal education did become more unpopular in England than in other parts of the United Kingdom, and in many other parts of the world, such unpopularity arose partly from the failure of those who controlled the education system to consider seriously the views of the majority of its consumers.

Just as in the British Empire beyond the seas education was provided for peoples of other nations and races with little or no regard for their cultures and priorities, so, too, in England, the same attitude was adopted towards the children and adults of what were described as the 'lower classes'.

Legislation of the twentieth century included some recognition of consumers. For example, the 1902 and 1921 Acts made provision for representations from parents about the supply of new schools. The latter also specifically recognized that the parental responsibility to secure efficient education might be exercised at home rather than in school. This was confirmed by the 1944 Act which stated that 'it shall be the duty of the parent of every child of compulsory school age to cause him to receive efficient full-time education suitable to his age, ability and aptitude, either by regular attendance at school or otherwise'. But ultimate power now lay with the providers. Parental consumers continued to have duties but few rights. This was confirmed by section 76 of the 1944 Act which, although it required the Minister of Education and local education authorities to 'have regard to the general principle . . . that pupils are to be educated in accordance with the wishes of their parents', so qualified this requirement by the further phrase 'in so far as is compatible with efficient instruction and training and the avoidance of unreasonable public expenditure', as to render the general principle meaningless.[14]

Even in the second half of the twentieth century many of the reasons which had led working–class parents to pay for the private schooling of their children a century before still applied. The priorities of secondary modern schools, their teachers, curricula and ethos, were abhorrent to many pupils and their parents. The Newsom Report of 1963 acknowledged that many secondary school children of average and below average ability were bored and apathetic, and saw little point in their schooling.

> Too many at present seem to sit through lessons with information and exhortation washing over them and leaving very little deposit. Too many appear to be bored and apathetic in school, as some will be in their jobs also. Others are openly impatient. They 'don't see the point' of what they are asked to do, they are conscious of making little progress . . . A headmaster acknowledges, 'There are far too many of our slow and average children who long ago reached saturation point doing tedious and hateful work year after year.'[15]

This situation was confirmed by the findings of Schools Council Enquiry I, *Young School Leavers*, published in 1968, which revealed sharp differences between what parents and pupils on the one hand, and teachers and head teachers on the other, saw as the function of education:

> Parents of 15 year old leavers almost universally saw as very important functions of the schools the teaching of things which would enable their child to obtain as good a job as possible and the imparting of the basic skills of being able to write correctly and to speak well and easily . . .
>
> The aims most widely seen by teachers as of great importance were the devel-

opment of pupils' characters and personalities, helping them to become independent and able to stand on their own feet, teaching about right and wrong, showing them how to behave so that they would be confident and at ease when they left school, teaching them how to speak well and easily and helping them in their personal relationships.[16]

Essentially, working-class children and their parents wanted sound instruction in basic subjects, vocational preparation and examination qualifications. In contrast the aims of teachers and head teachers seemed nebulous in the extreme.

Fears as to the exclusion of parents and other consumers from the education process were fuelled by studies such as this, and by the raising of the school leaving age to 16 in 1972. Concerns about primary education reached a peak with the much-publicized case of William Tyndale Junior School, which from 1973 under a new head teacher faced increasing problems. The Auld Report of 1976 showed that the ILEA, its administrators and advisers, and the school managers had been unable to prevent the virtual collapse of much of the education at the school.

In his Ruskin College speech of 1976, James Callaghan called for an increased role for parents, but it was the Conservative government of 1979, under Margaret Thatcher, which embraced the issue wholeheartedly. Parents and employers were consumers in a producer-dominated market and it was necessary to increase their role in order to improve the quality of the service – an argument which fitted well with a Conservative political philosophy which emphasised the importance of the free market, competition and efficiency. Two means of empowering the parental consumer were pursued – the first to give parents a significant presence on school governing bodies, the second to increase parental choice of schools.

In the nineteenth century, managers of elementary schools would not typically have included amongst their numbers parents of the pupils who attended them. From 1870 some school boards appointed management bodies, but others ran schools directly themselves. Management bodies of voluntary schools tended to be composed of representatives of the particular religious group with which they were associated. Although maintained secondary schools from 1902, in accordance with the traditional practice of grammar and public schools, usually had individual boards of governors, even after 1944 in some parts of the country, for example in twenty of the seventy-eight English county boroughs, the local education authority nominated a single governing body to control all its schools.

The Taylor Report of 1977 recommended that each school should have its own governing body, with equal representation of local education authority, teachers, parents and local community. The Education Act of 1980 gave parents some rights of representation on school governing bodies, but by the middle of the decade Conservative proposals as outlined in *Parental Influence at School* (1984) and *Better Schools* (1985) suggested that parents would be given an absolute majority on governing bodies. Opposition to these proposals, not least from parents themselves, led to the compromise of the Education (No. 2) Act of 1986 which produced a balanced composition of the type outlined in the Taylor Report. Under the 1988 Act considerable powers were accorded to these reconstituted governing bodies. Consumer power was not only increased by parental (and other local) membership of governing bodies. The rights of parents to information about the performance of the school and of their children enhanced their ability to call the governors (and ultimately local education authorities and central government) to account. In 1995 parents had the right to five types of information: reports from OFSTED; performance tables in respect of such issues as examination passes and truancy; school prospectuses; annual reports from school governors; annual or more frequent reports on their child's progress. They also, by means of a parental ballot, had the right to determine whether a maintained school should become grant-maintained.

Such information not only enabled parents, as consumers, to identify some of the weaknesses and problems of individual schools and local education authorities, it also brought into clearer relief those weaknesses and problems that result from the action, or inaction, of central government.

Choice is one of the most significant attributes attached to consumers in a market economy. Although, in the twentieth century, access to certain types of education, for example secondary schools and universities, was substantially increased, choice remained limited by such traditional factors as sex, wealth, ability and location. From the 1960s there was a general consumer revolution which was reflected in education by the emergence of such bodies as the Campaign for State Education (CASE), and various pro-comprehensive and grammar school lobbies. It also led to the establishment of councils with pupil representation in some schools, and student presence on committees and governing bodies in institutions of higher education. Overall, however, the advent of secondary comprehensive schooling appeared to place further restrictions upon choice. The coming of the neighbourhood school meant that parental choice would be exercised to a greater extent than before by choice of residence. One of the most radical schemes for promoting choice was that of a voucher system, advocated by Rhodes Boyson and others in the 1970s. Under this system parents would be given a voucher equal to the cost of education at a maintained school, which they could spend in the school of their choice, whether maintained or independent.

The Education Act of 1980 signalled the new Conservative government's limited commitment to the ideal of choice. Section 6 gave parents the right to express a preference for schools for their children, including voluntary schools and those in another local education authority, and section 7, the right of appeal to a legally constituted local appeals committee in cases of rejection. These sections, coupled with others on the rights of parents to information about schools, constituted the origins of the Parent's Charter. Another aspect of choice provided by the 1980 Act was the assisted places scheme, which supplied scholarships to independent schools for able pupils whose parents could not otherwise have afforded the fees.

Keith Joseph, who became Secretary for State for Education in 1981, was strongly attracted by the idea of vouchers.

> The voucher system would create pressure for standards to rise. I believe that there would be an increase in the number of good popular independent schools. I believe that if vouchers were combined with open enrolment, some of the least

good state schools would disappear, and increased competition might galvanize some of the less good state schools to achieve better results. These are the prospects that attract me to a combination of the voucher idea and open enrolment.[17]

In 1983 the voucher scheme was abandoned. Five years later the 1988 Act provided many of the elements of a voucher scheme – a greater variety of schools, more independence from local education authority control and open enrolment, but without the vouchers. The idea, however, is not dead, and may be applied to nursery, further or higher education in the first instance.

CONCLUSION

Four conclusions may be drawn from the historical perspective.

The first is to note that the role of consumers in education has been neglected: so, too, have the roles of those who provided private education. An even greater omission has been the neglect of provision and consumption of education within the family. Emphasis has been placed upon the rise of a publicly funded national system of education, with domestic, private and independent schooling seen either as an irrelevance or as the preserve of a wealthy and privileged minority. Yet although for much of English history a substantial proportion of formal educational institutions have been under the direct or indirect control of Church or state, much private teaching which involved a direct financial relationship between producer and consumer also existed, in domestic, occupational and religious contexts, as well as in schools. This was so in respect of a considerable minority of schools for children of the working classes in the nineteenth century and for the great majority of schools for the middling and upper classes.

A second conclusion relates to the nature of producers and consumers. The historical record shows that these two functions have frequently been intertwined. For example, since the middle ages the Christian Church has provided education for the express purpose of acting as a consumer of the products of such education – either in a specific sense as priests, monks or nuns, or in a general sense as adherents to the faith. Similarly, apprenticeship was provided by employers for the purpose of utilizing such youthful labour, of providing a steady source of recruits to the trade or profession, and of maintaining standards. Central government's interventions in educational matters have reflected similar concerns: a supply of skilled administrators; the production of good citizens. Another indication of the complexity of the relationship between producers and consumers is provided by the extent to which, over the centuries, prestigious educational producers – universities, public and private schools – have selected from a number of would-be consumers of their products. Choice has been exercised by the producer rather than by the consumer.

During the nineteenth century the rights of some consumers of education were drastically diminished. The previous freedom of working-class parental consumers to make choices about schools, curricula and patterns of attendance were removed, or very seriously curtailed. The theory developed that while some educational consumers had the ability to choose wisely on behalf of their children and had the means so to do, others lacked both the ability and the means and must therefore accept what was provided for them. During the second half of the century a particular problem arose in respect of those working-class parents who opted to send their children to private schools. In so doing they demonstrated their ability to choose and the means to do so. Their choices, however, were overridden by the power of central government which maintained that it understood the interests and needs of the majority of educational consumers better than they did themselves. This situation continued into the twentieth century.

Although there was considerable force in the argument that in educational matters some parents, like some children, were less perceptive judges of their long-term needs and interests than were teachers, or the officers of central and local government, by the second half of the twentieth century it was clear that there was a considerable mismatch between the expectations of many children and parents on the one hand, and what was being provided in schools on the other. This situation was exacerbated by the hierarchical nature of English secondary schools. There were insufficient places in the prestigious schools for those who wished to attend them, while other schools to which pupils were assigned were widely regarded, both by those who attended them and those who did not, as being seriously deficient. Legislation since 1980 has increased the power of consumers in relation to those of local education authorities, schools and teachers, but has reduced their powers in relation to those of central government. Parental choice, as construed by the Conservative government of Margaret Thatcher, did not include the choice to retain the ILEA. Nor did it allow much freedom of curricular choice during the years of compulsory schooling in maintained schools. The power of local education authorities and governing bodies to increase the expenditure of public money on schools was severely limited.

Finally, it may be argued that although the language and practices of the marketplace, including the concepts of producers and consumers, have been applied to education in recent years with some benefits, not least in respect of greater parental involvement in maintained schools, such languages and practices have their limitations. In urban areas where there are many schools, expectations that all parents will be able to send their children to the 'best' school in the town are clearly unrealistic. In rural areas choice may be severely limited by the fact that there is only one school within reasonable travelling distance. The relationship of those engaged in education is better understood as a partnership or contract, in which all have duties as well as rights. Such a partnership, as the evidence from nineteenth-century private schools for the wealthy and working classes suggests, is most likely to prosper in situations where there is broad agreement about the aims, content and methods of education.

NOTES

1. *The Times,* 27 November 1991.
2. *Independent,* 7 April 1992.
3. *The Times,* 17 March 1995.
4. *The Times,* 2 August 1991.
5. *National Commission Report,* 1993, 379.
6. *The Times,* 17 March 1995.
7. *The Times,* 31 December 1993.
8. *National Commission Briefings,* 1993, 183.
9. *Guardian,* 5 January 1993.
10. Gardner, 1984, 1.
11. Quoted in Aldrich, 1995, 72–3.
12. Quoted in Ball, 1983, 150.
13. Quoted in West, 1975, 37.
14. Quoted in Aldrich and Leighton, 1985, 45.
15. Quoted in Baron, 1965, 212.
16. Schools Council, 1968, 38, 41,
17. Quoted in Chitty, 1989, 184–5.

SUGGESTED READING

Adams, R. (1990) *Protests by Pupils: Empowerment, Schooling and the State.*
David, M. (1993) *Parents, Gender and Education Reform.*
Gardner, P. (1984) *The Lost Elementary Schools of Victorian England.*
Gordon. P. (1974) *The Victorian School Manager.*
Haviland, J. (1988) *Take Care, Mr Baker!*
Humphries, S. (1981) *Hooligans or Rebels?*
Silver, H. (1994) *Good Schools, Effective Schools.*

Conclusion

In a democratic state with universal adult suffrage the public education system comes under the ultimate ownership and control of the people. Nevertheless, as John Patten's question which formed the starting-point for this study implied, there is a general perception amongst the English that the formal public educational system is neither under popular control nor serving the best interests of the people. This situation may be contrasted with those in some other countries and, more immediately, in other parts of the United Kingdom. Such a contrast may be attributed to a variety of factors, including separate and more immediate political control, and the use of that control to conserve and promote distinctive elements of Scottish, Welsh and Irish culture.

BROAD AREAS

The seven chapters of this book have been based upon a carefully selected set of current educational issues, and each has begun with a discussion of such issues in their contemporary context. Subsequently, historical perspectives have been applied and conclusions drawn. These conclusions have been presented according to topics, but may now be regrouped into at least five broad areas: complexities, continuities, changes, the function of education, and historical perspectives themselves.

Today, educational issues are frequently presented in simple and confrontational terms. This tendency is exacerbated by the practices of television and the popular press, and of politicians. Yet, as the historical perspectives show, many educational issues are very complex indeed. For example, there is no simple division between producers and consumers in education. Parents, like schools, are both producers and consumers. Both parents and teachers also, on occasion, fulfil the roles of controllers and controlled. The control of education has at times been seen as a partnership, but it has also assumed the character of a contest between different groups, such as Church and state, teachers, parents and employers, who have formed different alliances at different points in history. It has also reflected partnerships and contests between different ideologies and ideals which have themselves been the product of wider social and political worlds. Substantial change in education has sometimes occurred when new alliances are formed between hitherto competing groups, or when one group forsakes its own particular interest in pursuit of what it believes to be a greater good.

Another example of complexity is to be found in the relationship between education and economic performance, a relationship that lies at the heart of much contemporary debate. Education may serve either as a means of investment, or of consumption. As the historical perspective demonstrates, improved national economic performance may at one time depend essentially upon economic factors, and on other occasions upon political or social ones – including those of general culture and of education.

Continuities in the English education system are also apparent. Not only have some educational institutions – for example the Universities of Oxford and Cambridge and some boys' public schools – enjoyed an unbroken existence since the middle ages, they have also retained their pre-eminent positions throughout those years. Continuities in the curricula of such institutions have also been apparent, while in the twentieth century itself, a reform that was presented as forward-looking, the National Curriculum of 1988, has been shown to be a virtual replica of that established under the secondary school regulations of 1904. Other continuities have been apparent in terms of teachers. For example, it would appear that the great majority of qualities deemed to be necessary in a good schoolteacher in the eighteenth century were very similar to those required in the twentieth.

But if there have been continuities, there have also been changes. There can be little doubt that twentieth-century England is more secular in educational, as in other, matters than it was a hundred years ago, and that the access of girls to formal education has increased over the same period. Such changes have been of a generally unidirectional nature, but other changes appear to have been rather cyclical or even backward-looking in character. For example, current emphasis upon school-based teacher training has many of the features of the apprenticeship model of the nineteenth century. Similarly, recent denigration of the role of local education authorities, and the prospect of their eventual elimination from the educational scene, conjures up the possibility of a return to the situation prior to the establishment of school boards in 1870. Changes of this type may reflect the contested nature of education, and the ascendancy of a particular group and ideology at a particular time. They may also reflect the fact that there is a fairly limited range of options in any particular situation. A change to apprenticeship or a reduction in the powers of local education authorities may not be a conscious decision to return to the prescriptions and methods of the mid-Victorian period, but rather change which can only be achieved by selecting from a very limited range of options – for example school- or college-based teacher training, or some combination of the two.

The function of education has also been characterized by continuities and changes. For much of English history the prime purpose of education was salvation, although attention was also paid to preparing young people for their adult roles in this life – as nobles and peasants, clerks and labourers, wives and mothers. The examination system, as developed from the second half of the nineteenth century, provided a limited means of social mobility via education, but also confirmed the broader function of the system as a means of selection. The reports of the Clarendon, Taunton and Newcastle Commissions reflected the divided nature of Victorian society and of its schools. The tripartite doctrine of the Norwood Report indicated the further divisions that were to bedevil maintained secondary schools in the twentieth century.

Finally, attention must be drawn to continuities and changes in the historical perspectives themselves. Much history of education has been written as Whig history, a history which charts a triumphal progress towards the present. The achievement of maintained elementary schooling for all in the nineteenth century and secondary schooling for all in the twentieth lay at the heart of this approach. But in recent years there have been significant attempts to modify this story. Brian Simon[1] has argued that the most significant feature of national education in England was its class-based and divisive nature, an interpretation which led him to champion secondary comprehensive schools. Phil Gardner[2] sought to rescue the private working-class schools of the nineteenth century from obloquy and oblivion, while Margaret Bryant,[3] Donald Leinster-Mackay[4] and John Roach[5] performed similar services for other types of private schools. The educational experiences of girls and women, both in formal and informal settings have also received much greater attention in recent years. In part these new perspectives stem from contemporary concerns. Historical investigation of such issues as private and public, as gender, as the relationship between education and economic performance, reflects the preoccupations of the present. It may well be followed by further consideration of such topics as consumers and producers, curriculum, methods of teaching and standards. But such historical investigation, in turn, has the power to reflect back upon the present and the future.

OWNERSHIP

Those reflections have been set forth in the conclusions to the seven chapters and now under five further groupings. Finally, one unifying theme, that of ownership, is taken to bring the historical perspective to bear upon understanding English education. As a concept ownership is all-inclusive. Ownership requires access and control; it encompasses teachers and other producers, as well as consumers. Curriculum and assessment constitute two of its primary concerns, as do investment in, and outcomes from, education, investment and outcomes which today are seen primarily in material rather than in moral and spiritual terms. In order that it may be fully explored two supplementary questions must be added in placing the issue of ownership of education in a broad historical context. Were there periods in English history when the perception of ownership was different from that of today, and, if so, how and why did such perceptions change?

The historical record shows that until the second half of the nineteenth century people in England did have a greater ownership of education than was the case in many other countries. It was widely believed, and the belief was as important as the fact, that the English generally enjoyed a range of freedoms which could be contrasted with the despotisms of other lands. Those freedoms, which had been won during the seventeenth-century war between King and Parliament, and consolidated, albeit in modified fashion, by the constitutional and religious settlement of 1688 and subsequent years, and the legislation of 1828 and 1829 which admitted both Protestant and Catholic Dissenters to political rights, extended to education. Though the report of the Newcastle Commission of 1861 criticized many aspects of schooling of the poor, it rejoiced in the fact that in England, where school attendance was not compulsory as it was in some other countries, nearly all children had some experience of schooling, usually as a result of the free choice of their parents or of themselves.

Why was this so? Within England, and to a lesser extent more broadly within Britain, there was a shared consciousness. This had a strong religious dimension, grounded in the Protestant Reformation of the sixteenth century which led to a greater emphasis upon a literate, as opposed to an oral and iconographic, culture. Particularly within England, such culture was linked to a national church. Another dimension (military and naval) of this shared consciousness came to prominence during the eighteenth century, principally as a result of wars in pursuit of empire and economic advantage against France in North America and India. The fortress mentality of unity against the peril of foreign Catholic domination by Spain in the sixteenth century, was reinforced in the eighteenth as French-supported Catholic Stuart pretenders were defeated in 1715 and 1745 by the generals of Hanoverian monarchs, and the might of Revolutionary and Napoleonic France subsequently held at bay.

During the nineteenth century the fortress mentality was relaxed as the size and power of the Empire and fleet seemed to assure that Britain was unassailable. National, constitutional, political, economic, religious and educational stability and superiority were taken for granted. In apparent contrast, on the European continent, France struggled with a succession of regimes, Italy and Germany experienced revolutions and national identity forged by force of arms, while Russian and Austrian emperors oscillated between repression and reform in ever more desperate attempts to control their increasingly ungovernable subjects. Of course there were shocks to British national pride and complacency. For example the inefficiency and mismanagement of the armed forces and of branches of the civilian administration, revealed by the Crimean War of 1854–56, was to be shown again in the South African War of 1899–1902, and compounded by the deaths of thousands of innocent civilians in concentration camps. Economic confidence was jolted by the poor performance of British products at the Paris Exhibition of 1867, and social consciences by revelations about poverty, malnutrition, homelessness and child prostitution in subsequent years.

Nevertheless, while the maintenance of the Protestant cause and the Church of England on the one hand, and the navy and army on the other, were seen to be legitimate areas of governmental concern, intervention in economic and social issues was less favourably viewed. Hence the reluctance of central government to establish state schools, and its preference for assisting voluntary, and subsequently local government, efforts. Government intervention was also hampered by the particular position of the Anglican church and by the rivalry, in matters of education as well as of faith, between the several Christian denominations. Divisions between those who wished to ensure the continuity of the privileged position of the Established Church in educational matters, and those who did not, were fundamental in preventing a more active role for the state in education. Even in respect of secular education, governments were reluctant to become too directly involved with education and training that promoted employment skills, for fear of upsetting the natural processes of economic competition. Government financial assistance was pitched at a minimum level. Just as it was argued that to make the workhouse too accommodating would induce poor people to abandon the search for an independent existence and resort to its shelter, so it was maintained that were state-assisted schools to become too successful, parents would not continue to finance independent schools. Free, compulsory schooling was widely seen as dangerous because it would seriously weaken the sense of responsibility which all parents should assume for the education of their children.

This meant that Victorian England had to rely upon an educational system which, in incidence, buildings and curricula still bore strong traces of its sixteenth-century origins. There were some important new common educational experiences, experiences which included children and adults of both sexes, and in which there was a mixture of social classes. Notable examples were the Sunday schools, some of which came under working-class control, and the mechanics' institutes and other independent adult educational movements, both secular and religious. But the most distinctive feature of these and other similar initiatives was that they were voluntary, part-time, and outside the main stream of the educational system that was consolidated in England from 1839, and particularly from 1862.

The people of England lost their ownership of education as a result of a series of changes which began in the second half of the nineteenth century, and were confirmed in the first half of the twentieth. The Newcastle Commissioners recommended a system of payment by results in order to circumvent the restrictions then in operation in respect of government grants to schools. Their aim was to ensure that most schools, and not just those under the control of the major societies, should be entitled to grants if their instruction was efficient, as tested by an annual examination. The proposed level of grant, moreover, was considerably higher than that actually imposed in 1862. Two further recommendations of this Commission were that a local rate should be levied by county boards of education, and that county inspectors should be chosen from amongst the ranks of teachers, those who actually had experience of teaching in elementary schools. None of these three recommendations was accepted. Central government grants were still restricted to a particular type of school, staffed by a particular type of teacher. Grants were fixed at a minimum level, and inspectors of schools continued to be recruited principally from amongst the ranks of graduates of Oxford and Cambridge, many of them in holy orders, some of whom, prior to their appointment, had never set foot in an elementary school.

Just as the Committee of Privy Council, established in 1839 to superintend public education, was a compromise arrangement, whereby powers over education were taken for the purpose of providing financial assistance to institutions owned by others, so the system established under the Revised Code of 1862 was an extension of that principle. The duty of central government was not seen as being to provide education, but rather to lay down terms upon which schools provided and owned by others could be assessed for the purpose of receiving government financial assistance. The Revised Code was a classic exercise in the centralization of power and the devolution of blame. Central government established the curriculum and the standards upon which government grants would be given. The inspectors of central government were the judges of those standards, and against their judgements it was both unwise and fruitless to appeal. Thus for the majority of elementary schools and schoolchildren, while the complex ownership of education was vested in a combination of managers, benefactors, teachers, even parents, the terms and conditions of such ownership were annually, for a period of but a few hours, submitted and subordinated to the agents of a central authority whose influence pervaded not only that day, but also (in consequence) every other school day throughout the year.

'My Lords' of the Privy Council, together with their overbearing officials and inspectors, were not committed to the establishment of a public education service in which all members of society might take pride and feel ownership. They were a race of superior and self-important beings whose attitude towards the teachers, parents and pupils who made use of the elementary school system, was invariably one of thinly disguised contempt. Little wonder that many parents continued to pay the full cost of their children's education at private working-class schools.

From 1870, the school boards, open to female electors and to female members, and with a sprinkling of working-class representation, promised to broaden the concept of public ownership of education. This broadening, which was not universal, for some areas were without school boards and in others the traditional owners of education, parson and squire, continued to dominate the rural boards, was matched by the loss of the private working-class school.

For most of the nineteenth century central government did not assist secondary education and, in spite of the urging of Matthew Arnold and others, such schools remained in the ownership of trustees, governors and private hands. In many cases, however, the grammar schools of England, which for centuries had served local communities, underwent significant changes. Some, including those specifically founded for the free education of local poor boys, became the preserves of the wealthy, by the simple expedient of excluding day boys and imposing substantial tuition and boarding fees. New foundations, including proprietary schools like Cheltenham College, owned by a group of shareholders who had the right to nominate pupils to the schools, were similarly independent from local or central public influence and control. In the last quarter of the century there was some broadening of ownership with the foundation of girls' grammar schools and the provision of scholarship places.

Although the local education authorities established under the 1902 Act were less numerous, and in some senses less democratic, than the school boards, they did provide a greater sense of public ownership of schooling, particularly in their secondary grammar schools. Ownership of the secondary school curriculum, however, remained principally with the Board of Education and with the universities through their examining boards. The large increase in numbers of educational professionals – both teachers and administrators – also provided a new group of potential owners of education.

The ideal of partnership and shared ownership formed part of the rhetoric that surrounded the 1944 Act, but less of the reality. Central government continued to supply direct financial support for higher education and for a handful of 'direct grant' schools. The ownership of the great majority of schools, however, rested with local education authorities who frequently maintained that their work was hampered by the inconsistent policies and financial restrictions of a Ministry which was as ineffective as the Board it had replaced. Children were assigned to different types of secondary schools with little regard for parental wishes. Grammar school places were few, and those children who might, indeed, have dealt more easily with concrete things than ideas, were generally denied access to technical schools. Secondary modern schools, to which the majority of children were consigned as 11-plus failures, were poorly resourced and of low status, schools from which, understandably, children sought to escape at the earliest possible opportunity. If these were the schools which three-quarters of the secondary age population of England and their parents were considered to 'own', then such ownership confirmed the continuation of nineteenth-century educational hierarchies into the twentieth. Popular ownership was denied. Secondary schooling for all was shown to be a hollow sham.

Some children from the working classes, and their parents, did want access to grammar schools, and some obtained it. But many more wanted access to schools which prepared them for public examinations in subjects that would be of direct use to them when seeking employment at age 16. Such schools might require greater, rather than lesser, funding per pupil than the grammar schools, for an effective technical, vocational and commercial education would need more resources than a bookish one. But in the years after 1945, ownership of secondary education remained firmly in the hands of the minority, rather than the majority of the English people. Though it would be quite wrong to decry the work and commitment of many secondary modern schools, their pupils and teachers, the great tragedy in terms of ownership was not that there were insufficient grammar school places, but that there were insufficient technical schools, and that secondary moderns were the also-rans of the system. This was not just the perception of parents and pupils. Teachers in such schools, and in primary schools, rightly felt that status and ownership in the profession belonged to those graduates in secondary grammar and independent schools who prepared pupils for public examinations.

Comprehensive secondary schools (though advocated by some as 'grammar schools for all') were one means of promoting the concept of a common school; GCSE of a common examination; the National Curriculum of a common core of study. Such developments were symptoms of the development of a sense of popular, as well as of individual, ownership of education. So, too, were increased participation rates in education, both post-16 and in higher education. Perceptions that local education authorities and teachers had acquired too much ownership of the maintained education system lay behind many of the educational reforms of the 1980s and 1990s. Those reforms led to an increase in ownership for governors, and particularly for parents, both in a governing and purely parental role. Grant-maintained status provided the opportunity for a new partnership of owners – teachers, parents and governors – with little or no ownership being exercised by the local education authority. But in 1994–95 only thirteen secondary schools voted to opt out of local education authority control, as opposed to more than 200 in each of the previous years, while only eighty-three primary schools became grant-maintained in contrast to 154 in 1993–94.[6]

Whilst many factors may lie behind such figures, it is clear that since 1839, and especially since 1870, public perception has been that central, rather than local, government has been the major impediment to a genuine public ownership of education. There is also a concern that, were local education authorities to be abolished completely, individual schools would have scant chance of withstanding central government policies, for example in terms of a reduction of funding. Of course, on occasion, local education authorities and teachers have been seen as assuming too great an influence, for example, by political packing of governing bodies on the one hand, or curriculum control and exclusion of parents from playgrounds and classrooms on the other. But educational reforms since 1979 have substantially weakened such influences and, in so doing, have exposed the role of central government itself. This has led to a resurgence of a feeling which has surfaced on several occasions during the last 150 years, that those who have presided over the national education system at central government level, both politicians and administrators, have too frequently pursued policies in which the genuine claims of the people of England to exercise a greater ownership over public education – in such matters as access, curriculum, standards, quality of teaching and outcomes – have been sacrificed to the demands of financial stringency and even to the interests of those whose children attend fee-paying schools.

Of course, for many decades the people of England have been divided by their educational experiences, particularly at secondary school level. In consequence only a small proportion of those whose children have attended maintained schools have exercised effective control. Nevertheless, in the nineteenth century many working-class parents did exercise considerable choice and ownership, not only over the education but also over the schooling, of their children. The most significant effect of recent educational reforms would be to enable them to do so again.

John Patten's question as to why people in this country feel that they do not own education is a most important one that lies not only at the heart of an understanding of English education, but also of the whole educational process. For education, as distinct from training, carries an implication of ownership on the part of the person being educated. Of course, many individuals and many groups in society have felt, and do feel, that they have ownership of education, for example, as a result of their ability to purchase a superior education for their offspring, as a consequence of their own successes within the formal educational system, as examples of self-education, as educational professionals. In contrast, many people, and, it could be argued, many more people, have not felt, and do not feel, that they have ownership of education for precisely the opposite reasons. They lack sufficient financial resources to purchase educational advantage for their children, they have not themselves enjoyed success within the formal sphere of education, they have little tradition or interest in self-education, and no direct experience as educational professionals.

How, then, may a greater sense of ownership of education be promoted? The answers are clear. First, by reducing (by means of a process of levelling up) those educational advantages which hitherto have been largely reserved to the children of the affluent. Second, by increasing opportunities for educational participation and success, including those which may broadly be described as self-education. Third, by forging a strong partnership between all engaged in education, whether as learners or teachers, lay or professional, a partnership which looks beyond immediate purposes to the more important end of promoting amongst the English a greater awareness of the worth both of the educated individual and of the educated nation.

NOTES

1. Simon, 1974.
2. Gardner, 1984.
3. Bryant, 1986.
4. Leinster-Mackay, 1984.
5. Roach, 1986, 1991
6. *The Times*, 4 April 1995.

Select Bibliography

(This Bibliography contains all references in the Notes, the Suggested Readings, together with a small number of other key works.)

Adams, R. (1991) *Protests by Pupils: Empowerment, Schooling and the State*. London: Falmer Press.

Aldcroft, D. (1992) *Education, Training and Economic Performance, 1944–1990*. Manchester: Manchester University Press.

Aldrich, R. (1982) *An Introduction to the History of Education*. London: Hodder and Stoughton.

Aldrich, R. (ed.) (1991) *History in the National Curriculum*. London: Kogan Page.

Aldrich, R. (1995) *Schools and Society in Victorian Britain: Joseph Payne and the New World of Education*. New York: Garland Press.

Aldrich, R. and Leighton, P. (1985) *Education: Time for a New Act?* London: Institute of Education, University of London.

Antal, A. B. (1990) *Making Ends Meet. Corporate Responses to Youth Unemployment in Great Britain and the Federal Republic of Germany*. London: Anglo-German Foundation.

Appleby, J., Hunt, L. and Jacob, M. (1994) *Telling the Truth About History*. New York: Norton.

Arnot, M. (1985) *Race and Gender: Equal Opportunities Policies in Education*. Oxford: Pergamon Press.

Ball, N. (1983) *Educating the People. A Documentary History of Elementary Schooling in England and Wales*. London: Temple Smith.

Barber, M. (1992) *Education and the Teacher Unions*. London: Cassell.

Barber, M. (ed.) (1992) *Education in the Capital*. London: Cassell.

Barnett, C. (1972) *The Collapse of British Power*. London: Eyre Methuen.

Baron, G. (1965) *Society, Schools and Progress in England*. Oxford: Pergamon.

Bell, R., Fowler, G. and Little, K. (eds) (1973) *Education in Great Britain and Ireland: a Source Book*. London: Routledge and Kegan Paul.

Benson, C. and Silver, H. (1991) *Vocationalism in the United Kingdom and the United States*. London: Post-16 Centre, Institute of Education, University of London.

Benton, L. and Noyelle, T. (1992) *Adult Illiteracy and Economic Performance*. Paris: OECD.

Bernbaum, G. (ed.) (1979) *Schooling in Decline*. London: Macmillan.

Bishop, A. S. (1971) *The Rise of a Central Authority for English Education*. Cambridge: Cambridge University Press.

Blaug, M. (1970) *An Introduction to the Economics of Education*. London: Allen Lane.

Brooks, R. (1991) *Contemporary Debates in English Education: An Historical Perspective*. London: Longman.

Bryant, M. (1986) *The London Experience of Secondary Education*. London: Athlone Press.

Calderhead, J. (ed.) (1987) *Exploring Teachers' Thinking*. London: Cassell.

Calderhead, J. (ed.) (1988) *Teachers' Professional Learning*. London: Falmer Press.

Castle, E. B. (1970) *The Teacher*. Oxford: Oxford University Press.

Chapman, J. V. (1985) *Professional Roots. The College of Preceptors in British Society*. Theydon Bois: Theydon Bois Publications.

Chitty, C. (1989) *Towards a New Education System: the Victory of the New Right?* London: Falmer Press.

Cordingley, P. and Kogan, M. (1993) *In Support of Education: the Functioning of Local Government*. London: Jessica Kingsley Publishing.

Cotgrove, S. F. (1958) *Technical Education and Social Change*. London: Allen and Unwin.

Cressy, D. (1975) *Education in Tudor and Stuart England*. London: Edward Arnold.

David, M. (1980) *The State, the Family and Education*. London: Routledge and Kegan Paul.

David, M. (1993) *Parents, Gender and Education Reform*. Cambridge: Polity Press.

Dent, H. C. (1977) *The Training of Teachers in England and Wales, 1800–1975*. London: Hodder and Stoughton.

Department of Education and Science (1983) *Teaching Quality*. London: HMSO.

Dyhouse, C. (1981) *Girls Growing Up in Late Victorian and Edwardian England*. London: Routledge and Kegan Paul.

Findlay, J. J. (1902) *Principles of Class Teaching*. London: Macmillan.

Fisher, P. (1982) *External Examinations in Secondary Schools in England, 1944–1964*. Leeds: University of Leeds.

Floud, R. and McCloskey, D. (eds) (1981) *The Economic History of Britain since 1700*. 2 vols. Cambridge: Cambridge University Press.

Gardner, P. (1984) *The Lost Elementary Schools of Victorian England: the People's Education*. London: Croom Helm.

Gipps, C. and Stobart, G. (1993) *Assessment: a Teachers' Guide to the Issues*. London: Hodder and Stoughton.

Goldstrom, J. M. (1972) *Education: Elementary Education, 1780–1900*. Newton Abbot: David and Charles.

Goodson, I. (ed.) (1985) *Social Histories of the Secondary Curriculum*. London: Falmer Press.

Goodson, I. and Ball, S. (eds) (1984) *Defining the Curriculum: Histories and Ethnographies*. London: Falmer Press.

Gordon, P. (1974) *The Victorian School Manager: a Study in the Management of Education, 1800–1902*. London: Woburn Press.

Gordon, P. (1980) *Selection for Secondary Education*. London: Woburn Press.

Gordon, P. (ed.) (1983) *Is Teaching a Profession?* London: Institute of Education, University of London.

Gordon, P. and Lawton, D. (1978) *Curriculum Change in the Nineteenth and Twentieth Centuries*. London: Hodder and Stoughton.

Gosden, P. H. J. H. (1966) *The Development of Educational Administration in England and Wales*. Oxford: Blackwell.

Gosden, P. H. J. H. (1969) *How They Were Taught. An Anthology of Contemporary Accounts of Learning and Teaching in England 1800–1950*. Oxford: Blackwell.

Gosden, P. H. J. H. (1972) *The Evolution of a Profession*. Oxford. Blackwell.

Gosden, P. H. J. H. (1983) *The Education System since 1944*. Oxford: Martin Robertson.

Gosden, P. H. J. H. and Sharp, P. R. (1978) *The Development of an Education Service: the West Riding, 1889–1974*. Oxford: Martin Robertson.

Graham, D. (with Tytler, D.) (1993) *A Lesson for Us All: the Making of the National Curriculum*. London: Routledge.

Graves, N. (ed.) (1990) *Initial Teacher Education: Policies and Progress*. London: Kogan Page.

Green, A. (1990) *Education and State Formation: the Rise of Education Systems in England, France and the USA*. London: Macmillan.

Green, A. and Steedman, H. (1993) *Educational Provision, Educational Attainment and the Needs of Industry: a Review of Research for Germany, France, Japan, the USA and Britain*. London: National Institute of Economic and Social Research.

Guagnini, A. (1993) 'Worlds apart: academic instruction and professional qualifications in the training of mechanical engineers in England, 1850–1914', in Fox, R. and Guagnini, A. (eds) *Education, Technology and Industrial Performance in Europe, 1850–1939*. Cambridge: Cambridge University Press.

Haft, H. and Hopmann, S. (eds) (1990) *Case Studies in Curriculum Administration History*. London: Falmer Press.

Halsey, A. H., Heath, A. F. and Ridge, J. M. (1980) *Origins and Destinations. Family, Class and Education in Modern Britain*. Oxford: Clarendon Press.

Haviland, J. (1988) *Take Care, Mr Baker!* London: Fourth Estate.

Hennock, E. (1990) 'Technological education in England, 1850–1926: the uses of a German model', *History of Education*, 19,4.

Heward, C. (1988) *Making a Man of Him. Parents and their Sons' Education at an English Public School*. London: Routledge.

History of Education Society (1970) *Studies in the Government and Control of Education*. London: Methuen.

Hough, J. R. (1987) *Education and the National Economy*. London: Croom Helm.

Humphries, S. (1981) *Hooligans or Rebels? An Oral History of Working-Class Childhood and Youth, 1889–1939*. Oxford: Basil Blackwell.

Hunt, F. (1991) *Gender and Policy in English Education: Schooling for Girls 1902–44*. New York: Harvester Wheatsheaf.

Jackson, B. (1964) *Streaming: an Education System in Miniature*. London: Routledge and Kegan Paul.

John, G. (1992) 'Education and the Community in a Metropolis' in Barber, M. (ed.), *Education in the Capital*. London: Cassell.

Jones, L. G. E. (1924) *The Training of Teachers in England and Wales: a Critical Survey*. Oxford: Oxford University Press.

Kazamias, A. (1966) *Politics, Society and Secondary Education in England*. Philadelphia: University of Pennsylvania Press.

Kay-Shuttleworth, J. (1839) *Recent Measures for the Promotion of Education in England*. London. Ridgway.

Kyriacou, C. (1992) *Effective Teaching in Schools*. Hemel Hempstead: Simon and Schuster.

Lauglo, J. and McLean, M. (eds) (1985) *The Control of Education. International Perspectives on the Centralization-Decentralization Debate*. London: Heinemann.

Lawton, D. (1975) *Class, Culture and the Curriculum*. London: Routledge and Kegan Paul.

Lawton, D. and Chitty, C. (eds) (1988) *The National Curriculum*. London: Institute of Education, University of London.

Leinster-Mackay, D. P. (1984) *The Rise of the English Prep School*. London: Falmer.

Lester Smith, W. O. (1945) *To Whom do Schools Belong?* Oxford: Basil Blackwell.

Lester Smith, W. O. (1965) *Government of Education*. Harmondsworth: Penguin.

Lewis, L. J. (1961) *Days of Learning: an Anthology of Passages from Autobiography for Student Teachers*. Oxford: Oxford University Press.

Lomax, D. (ed.) (1973) *The Education of Teachers in Britain*. London: Wiley.

Maclure, J. S. (1969) *Educational Documents, England and Wales 1816–1968*. London: Methuen.

Maclure, J. S. (1970) 'The control of education', in History of Education Society, *Studies in the Government and Control of Education*. London: Methuen.

McCarthy, J. (1988) *Educating for Decline? British Economic Performance and the Education System*. Worcester: Worcester College of Higher Education.

McCulloch, G. (1989) *The Secondary Technical School: a Usable Past?* London: Falmer Press.

Mathews, J. (1985) *Examinations: a Commentary*. London: Allen and Unwin.

Mathias, P. (1983) *The First Industrial Nation. An Economic History of Britain, 1700–1914*. London: Methuen.

Minshull, G. N. (1990) *The New Europe. An Economic Geography of Europe in the 1990s*. London: Hodder and Stoughton.

Mitchell, B. R. and Deane, P. (1962) *Abstract of British Historical Statistics*. Cambridge: Cambridge University Press.

Montgomery, R. (1965) *Examinations. An Account of their Evolution as Administrative Devices in England*. London: Longmans.

Montgomery, R. (1978) *A New Examination of Examinations*. London: Routledge and Kegan Paul.

Murphy, J. (1971) *Church, State and Schools in Britain, 1800–1970*. London: Routledge and Kegan Paul.

Naish, M. (1990) 'Teacher education today', in Graves, N. (ed.), *Initial Teacher Education. Policies and Progress*. London: Kogan Page.

National Commission on Education (1993) *Briefings*. London: Heinemann.

National Commission on Education (1993) *Learning to Succeed*. London: Heinemann.

OECD (1993) *Curriculum Reform: Assessment in Question*. Paris: OECD.

OFSTED (1993) *Access and Achievement in Urban Education*. London: HMSO.

Parker, I. (1914) *Dissenting Academies in England*. Cambridge: Cambridge University Press.

Prais, S. J. and Wagner, K. (1985) 'Schooling standards in England and Germany: some summary comparisons bearing on economic performance', *National Institute Economic Review*, 112.

Purvis, J. (1991) *A History of Women's Education in England*. Milton Keynes: Open University Press.

Randlesome, C., Brierley, W., Bruton, K., Gordon, D. and King, P. (1990) *Business Cultures in Europe*. Oxford: Heinemann.

Rattansi, A. and Reeder, D. (eds) (1992) *Rethinking Radical Education. Essays in Honour of Brian Simon*. London: Lawrence and Wishart.

Reeder, D. (ed.) (1980) *Educating Our Masters*. Leicester: Leicester University Press.

Regan, D, (1979) *Local Government and Education*. London: Allen and Unwin.

Rich, R. W. (1972) *The Training of Teachers in England and Wales during the Nineteenth Century*. Bath: Cedric Chivers.

Roach, J. (1971) *Public Examinations in England, 1850–1900*. London: Cambridge University Press.

Roach, J. (1986) *A History of Secondary Education in England, 1800–1870*. London: Longman.

Roach, J. (1991) *Secondary Education in England, 1870–1902: Public Activity and Private Enterprise*. London: Routledge.

Roberts, K., Dench, S. and Richardson, D. (1988) 'Youth unemployment in the

1980s', in Coles, B. (ed.) *Young Careers: The Search for Jobs and the New Vocationalism*. Milton Keynes: Open University Press.

Roderick, G. W. and Stephens, M. D. (1978) *Education and Industry in the Nineteenth Century: the English Disease*. London: Longman.

Roderick, G. W. and Stephens, M. D. (eds) (1982) *The British Malaise. Industrial Performance and Training in Britain today*. London: Falmer Press.

Rubinstein, W. D. (1993) *Capitalism, Culture and Decline in Britain, 1750–1990*. London: Routledge.

Sanderson, M. (1972) *The Universities and British Industry, 1850–1970*. London: Routledge and Kegan Paul.

Sanderson, M. (1987) *Educational Opportunity and Social Change in England*. London: Faber and Faber.

Sanderson, M. (1994) *The Missing Stratum: Technical School Education in England, 1900–1990s*. London: Athlone Press.

School Curriculum and Assessment Authority (1994) *The National Curriculum and its Assessment*. London: SCAA.

Schools Council (1968) *Young School Leavers*. London: HMSO.

Selleck, R. J. W. (1968) *The New Education: the English Background, 1870–1914*. Melbourne: Pitman.

Selleck, R. J. W. (1972) *English Primary Education and the Progressives, 1914–1939*. London: Routledge and Kegan Paul.

Sharp, P. and Dunford, J. (1990) *The Education System in England and Wales*. London: Longman.

Silver, H. (ed.) (1973) *Equal Opportunity in Education*. London: Methuen.

Silver, H. (1994) *Good Schools, Effective Schools. Judgements and their Histories*. London: Cassell.

Simon, B. (1974) *The Two Nations and the Educational Structure, 1780–1870*. London: Lawrence and Wishart.

Simon, B. (1994) *The State and Educational Change: Essays in the History of Education and Pedagogy*. London: Lawrence and Wishart.

Smelser, N. (1991) *Social Paralysis and Social Change. British Working-Class Education in the Nineteenth Century*. Berkeley: University of California Press.

Steedman, H. and Green, A. (1993) *Educational Achievement in Britain, France, Germany and Japan. A Comparative Analysis*. London: Post-16 Centre, Institute of Education, University of London.

Stone, M. (1985) *The Education of the Black Child: the Myth of Multiracial Education*. London: Fontana.

Sutherland, G. (1971) *Elementary Education in the Nineteenth Century*. London: Historical Association.

Sutherland, G. (1984) *Ability, Merit and Measurement. Mental Testing and English Education, 1880–1940*. Oxford: Clarendon.

Sylvester, D. (1970) *Educational Documents 800–1816*. London: Methuen.

Talbott, J. (1707) *The Christian Schoolmaster*. London: Joseph Downing.

Tomlinson, J. (1993) *The Control of Education*. London: Cassell.

Tosh, J. (1984) *The Pursuit of History*. London: Longman.

Tropp, A. (1957) *The School Teachers*. London: Heinemann.

Vaizey, J. (1963) *The Control of Education*. London: Faber and Faber.

West, E. G. (1975) *Education and the Industrial Revolution*. London: Batsford.

White, R. and Brockington, D. (1983) *Tales Out Of School: Consumers' View of British Education*. London: Routledge and Kegan Paul.

Wiener, M. J. (1981) *English Culture and the Decline of the Industrial Spirit, 1850–1980*. Cambridge: Cambridge University Press.

Wiseman, S. (1961) *Examinations and English Education*. Manchester: Manchester University Press.

Worswick, G. (ed.) (1985) *Education and Economic Performance*. Aldershot: Gower Publishing.

Wragg, E. C. (1974) *Teaching Teaching*. Newton Abbot: David and Charles.

Wragg, E. C. (1982) *A Review of Research in Teacher Education*. Windsor: NFER-Nelson.

Wragg, E. C. (1984) *Classroom Teaching Skills*. London: Croom Helm.

Index